DIVING
FOR
FUN

A Complete Textbook for Students, Instructors, and
Advanced Divers

by

Joe Strykowski

Illustrations by Ernie Duerksen

DACOR CORPORATION

FOREWORD

Over the years, since we manufactured our first regulator, we have had the good fortune to meet many fine diving instructors throughout the world. We have been singularly impressed with one outstanding trait which seems to be common to most of these dynamic personalities.

That trait is dedication!

Whether certified by the Y.M.C.A., N.A.U.I., N.A.S.D.S., P.A.D.I., S.S.I. or L.A. County, the diving instructor is dedicated to the safety and growth of this sport and frankly, the industry could not exist without him.

There have been a number of diving texts written and each has served immeasurably well in training countless thousands of our present crop of diving enthusiasts. But we couldn't help but feel that there was need for a new diving textbook; one which would encompass current advancements and which would, at the same time, provide the comprehensive information demanded by today's student-diver.

The requirements were rigid.

The book would have to be stripped of the ever present "sea stories" and other superfluous prose. It would have to be concise and clearly written to remove the mystique which always manages to creep into such books. Finally, it would have to be written in a manner which would satisfy the requirements of all instructional programs.

It was for these reasons that we asked Joe Strykowski to author such a book and we are proud and privileged to present the work written by this eminent diver, instructor and writer.

All of our staff have read DIVING FOR FUN, and we feel, as does he, that safety under water is the sum total of knowledge and experience. We believe that DIVING FOR FUN will help provide that knowledge. The experience will take care of itself.

Sam Davison, *President*
Dacor Corporation

CONTENTS

Chapter 1   DIVING FOR FUN

The diver is free.

When he seals the mask over his face and molds the mouthpiece to his lips and descends, the diver and his buddy are on their own.

They can go exactly where they choose, exploring all compass points underwater for there is no one to say they shall not. Only the diver knows the peace of mind it brings. The diver is free.

The non-diver stands landlocked at the edge of the sea and views the seemingly endless vista of blue skies and sunlit water. He cannot conceive the excitement, the peace, or the beauty of that which lies hidden from his eyes. Magnificent canyons and valleys, vast deserts of pale blue sand, enchanted forests of dwarfed trees and exploding colors and shapes reveal themselves only to the diver's eyes. The underwater world is waiting.

There are few adventures left in this world as fascinating or as productive of the good in man as diving.

DIVING FOR FUN attempts to collect within its pages the basic principles of this art.

Knowledge of the art has been acquired over the years through the efforts of hundreds of diving enthusiasts, many of whom have devoted their lives to that study.

Over the last decade a number of excellent manuals have been prepared by some eminently qualified divers, many of whom have been summoned to the ranks of the newly developing ocean industries. The commercialization of the underwater world has taken precedence over the sport, as well it should.

But industry's gain has not been the sport's loss entirely.

The colonization of the sea floor is providing new and advanced information at a rate so fast that it is impossible for diver's textbooks to stay abreast.

The dogma of yesterday is obsoleted by today's new and exciting advances and hopefully even seasoned divers will find something in these pages to while away a rainy afternoon.

This book has but one purpose — to provide the student-diver with information which will enable him to dive with greater safety. Hopefully, it will serve as a source of information from which he may draw at anytime for his own increased proficiency.

If your interests lie in the direction of mixed gas diving, salvage diving, or underwater photography; then you need extensive specialized training and you have progressed beyond the scope of this book.

Diving is a remarkable teacher.

It teaches self-confidence to the meek and humility to the bold, initiative to the withdrawn and philosophy to all.

It teaches you to take infinite pains and builds character, determination and cool judgement.

Mention should be made of the camaraderie in the diving fraternity. Diving provides an adventure that binds its devotees together by a common sense of responsibility for one another's safety.

It brings out the finest qualities in man and results in the most enduring of friendships.

There are four ultra-important requisites to a safe and confident diving career. They are JUDGMENT, ATTITUDE, DISCIPLINE and FITNESS.

1

Requisites for A Safe Diving Career

their knowledge beyond the material presented in this book. For them, we have provided a list of recommended books in the appendix.

DISCIPLINE

This generally means acting in accordance with the rules or having yourself under control at all times. Are you an attentive diver who systematically plans a dive, or do you go bopping off across the sea floor and end up surfacing miles down current from your dive boat? Discipline can be most difficult at times. It's difficult to abide by the safety rules when only one more nut holds the ship's bell to the bulkhead of that sunken wreck — but be firm! In the final analysis, discipline simply means developing a mature approach to diving.

FITNESS

Just as there are no substitutes for judgement, discipline, and attitude, neither is there a substitute for a high degree of physical fitness. Sport diving doesn't demand great strenth, but in an emergency the diver's endurance, his ability to withstand heavy exertion, may be tested. Emotional stability is also of paramount importance, for it is stability which enables the

JUDGMENT

There is no substitute for common sense and surprisingly, once the fundamentals of diving are digested, common sense dictates your procedures underwater. The scuba instructor won't be upset over your not being the smoothest diver on the beach. But if you don't exhibit common sense and wander away from your buddy, or simply ignore the safety rules, you'll have a rough time finding anyone to dive with you.

The use of good judgment in both the planning and the carrying out of your dives will reward you with many years of safe and exciting adventure.

ATTITUDE

Resign yourself to following the scuba instructor's advice. If you're really interested in safe diving, you'll work hard and make a sincere effort to learn. If you do, the instructor will pull out all stops to help even if you goof occasionally.

This book will help to provide that knowledge.

Most divers will not be content with passing a basic scuba course. They will want to extend

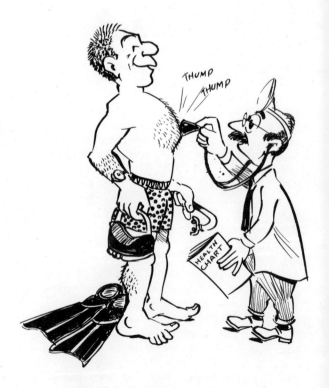

There Is No Substitute For Fitness

diver to handle the emergency. Learning to dive is so easy that even the fellow "out of condition" may be lulled into dangerous complacency. Nobody should participate in sport diving without a thorough physical examination. A medical examination form designed specifically for sport divers is included in the appendix of this book.

WATERMANSHIP

There seem to be two popular misconceptions regarding the level of swimming ability necessary for safe sport diving:

a) one must be an olympic swimmer and,

b) one needn't even know how to swim since the equipment makes a diver.

Neither is true, of course. If you can complete the following Y.M.C.A. swimming proficiency tests and are comfortable in the water, you're ready.

1. Tread water for 3 minutes, using feet only.
2. Swim 300 yards.
3. Tow an inert swimmer 40 yards.
4. Stay afloat 15 minutes.
5. Swim 15 yards underwater.

One caution remains for me to add. Although much can be learned from reading and study, no book can substitute for competent, supervised instruction.

This book coupled with the instruction of a certified diving instructor will provide you with the necessary skills to enjoy one of the most pleasurable experiences in the world. Experience along with these skills will make you a good diver.

". . . I am not at home, not in any city, or among any people. I am far out in the Pacific Ocean on a desert island, sitting on the bottom of the sea. I am deep underwater, at a spot where no human being has ever been before. This is one of the most important moments of my life."
Doctor William Beebe, *"Beneath Tropic Seas"*

Chapter 2 THE UNDERWATER WORLD

Those who leave behind the warmth and security of home to dive have discovered the breathtaking beauty of the underwater world and the friendliness and curiosity of its inhabitants.

Sometimes in their more tolerant moments they may even pity the poor, land-locked soul who still believes that this wonderous blue continent is a mysterious, never-never land hiding incalculable dangers and frightening sea monsters.

The diver must learn of the sea and its inhabitants. He must neither dismiss the shark as a coward, nor the lowly man-of-war as a subject unworthy of study. The sea has a greater diversity of the sixty classes of animal than even land can offer. In this book we are unfortunately compelled to discuss the hazardous marine life, which are a mere handful when compared to the millions of harmless sea animals.

The true dangers of the sea are passive.

The sun burns the unprotected diver.

The man-of-war and fire coral sting the unwary diver.

And the rip current may drown the untrained diver.

The most dangerous mistake the novice diver can make is to ignore these seemingly trivial aspects of the underwater world. He is to a large degree dependent upon the environment. He cannot change it, thank God, but if he studies the sea and respects her creatures, they will respect him.

KELP

A dive through the kelp forests of Southern California will leave the diver with an indelible impression of striking beauty.

The imaginative diver may feel himself tiptoeing through a cathedral, where subdued light

The True Dangers of the Sea Are Passive

slants down through imposing kelp trees reaching to the surface as much as 100 feet overhead. Curious eyes peer out at the diver from the labyrinth of tunnels formed by the thick kelp.

With the sea floor an anchor, air bladders float the kelp to the surface where it may fan out into a thick cover. The diver ascending into a heavy concentration could become seriously entangled should he try to push through to the surface.

The diver should surface slowly where the cover is lightest, parting the kelp with hands held overhead. Take a bearing on the closest open water, descend feet first, and swim underwater to the clear area.

One cannot power himself out of a kelp entanglement, it will only be made worse. If entangled, signal your buddy and calmly work out of it. The diver's knife would be of great value in such a situation.

5

SUN

It may seem pointless to discuss the painful consequences of ignoring the powers of the sun, but more diving trips into tropical waters end prematurely because of severe sun burns than might be imagined. The diver is particularly vulnerable to the sun. As the snorkeler paddles slowly about the reefs, captivated by the beauty of coral and fish, he has forgotten time and is unaware that his unprotected body is being burned. The water cools him but at the same time reflects the sun's rays, intensifying the burn.

Suntan oils and lotions are useless since the water washes them away. Make your first exposures to the sun brief, no more than 10 or 20 minutes at a time. During the first and second days in the sun country, the diver is most vulnerable to the hazards of the sun.

When out of the water, use protective sunscreening lotions and stay out of the sun. In the water, cover up with a long sleeved shirt with a high collar and trousers to protect your legs. You may look ridiculous in the water, but it beats suffering third degree sunburns. Some divers invest in dancer's leotards and tights which are quite handsome and exceptionally rugged. These are generally available from theatrical supply houses and should not be confused with the inexpensive, department store variety which tear easily and tend to sag unseemingly at the posterior.

Should you get a burn, use cooling ointments, stay out of the sun and rest. Aspirin taken judiciously will help regulate body temperature.

SURF

When the surf is running high the wise diver will postpone the dive until a better day. Entering the water in heavy surf can result in loss of equipment and possible injury.

When entering through surf, tie all equipment to an innertube which can be towed at a safe distance behind with a light nylon line.

Time the entrance for the interval between breakers; swim out with the waves back-surge, porpoising under the oncoming waves until quiet water is reached.

When leaving the water, remove your fins and swim in quickly with the light wave's until the water shallows enough to allow you to sprint to shore or, if exiting along a rocky shore, swim to where the surge is least noticeable and climb quickly beyond the reach of the next surge.

The best advice is to learn about local water conditions by diving with experienced divers of the area.

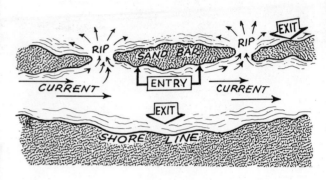

The Rip Current

RIP CURRENT

A rip current occurs when a water flow runs back out to sea through a narrow gap cut through an offshore sandbar or reef. Water flowing parallel to shore suddenly changes direction and flows seaward.

A diver caught in this current may be swept quickly out to sea at a speed greater than he is capable of swimming against.

If caught in a rip current, don't attempt to swim against it. Stay calm, inflate your vest, ditch your weight belt, and float with the current.

Rip currents are short-lived and dissipate quickly once beyond the reef gap. Conserve your strength and once free of the current, swim back to shore in a direction well clear of the rip current.

For safety's sake, before entering the water, observe the current action and carefully plan your points of entry and exit.

TIDAL CURRENT

Tidal currents result from tide changes and the wise diver plans his diving activities for periods of slack water. Tidal currents are consistent in many areas and are published in tide tables available to the sport diver.

When diving, stay upcurrent of your dive boat so that at the end of the dive, when you're likely to be a bit tired anyhow, you'll be able to drift effortlessly down toward the boat.

Living Pincushion

SEA URCHIN

The sea urchin has been called a "living pin-cushion" (as well as some other unprintable names) by unfortunate divers who have painfully discovered how sharp its long, brittle spines can be.

Depending upon the species, the spiny sea urchin may grow to a diameter of 10 inches and be covered with long, brittle spines or short, heavy spines. The sea urchin, common to all tropical waters, travels slowly across the ocean floor on small tube feet, stopping for long periods to scrape algae from coral for nourishment. In some areas, the sea urchin may litterally cover the sea floor and lodge even deep in crevices in a coral reef. If brushed against, stepped on, or sat upon, the spines may break off under the skin producing a painful puncture. Generally, the pain will quickly subside and the particles imbedded under the skin will dissolve in time.

CORAL

Claire Booth Luce, eminent writer, naturalist, and diving enthusiast was so moved by her first underwater visit to a coral reef, she wrote: "What fishes like flowers, what stones like trees. The coral reefs are a golden girdle of dead and living cities, which dwarf in their age and beauty all the cities of man."

A coral reef has been called the family tree in lime of the millions of polyps who had colonized, reproduced and died adding at death their substance to the increasing height and breadth of the coral. On any one stretch of reef the coral present may include a hundred different species ranging from staghorn and brain corals to the fragile, lace-work of the seafan.

Coral can be extremely sharp, and can cause seemingly superficial cuts, which if not immediately cared for may result in serious infections.

Fire coral grows in a variety of shapes and can produce a stinging sensation which has been described as "moderately" painful. Several years ago, while filming on a coral reef, I had the misfortune to brush against a large leaf of fire coral. To call the ensuing pain moderate would be tantamount to describing being run over by a fire engine as "moderately" painful. Large brown welts produced by the stinging didn't completely disappear for eight weeks!

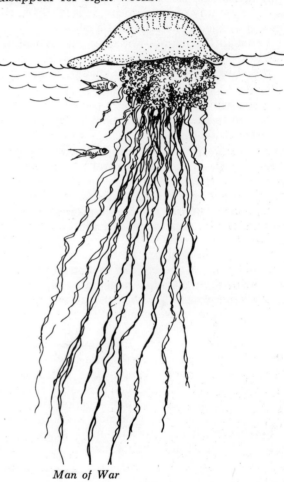

Man of War

PORTUGUESE MAN-OF-WAR

Of all the many fascinating creatures of the sea, the man-of-war is doubtless one of the least understood. We tend to speak of the man-of-war as one animal, when it is actually a floating colony of hundreds of individual polyps.

The man-of-war's gas filled float resembles an irridescent balloon tinted in shades of purple and blue. Topping the float is a crest-like sail extending fore and aft. Though the float rarely exceeds a length of 12 inches, its tentacles may extend as deep as 100 feet. Lining these tentacles are thousands of stinging cells (nematocysts) which are capable of paralyzing and killing fish many times larger than the man-of-war itself. The stinging cell consists of a long coiled tube and a stinger-like trigger. When touched the spring-loaded stinger is fired into the flesh and a paralyzing poison is injected through the tube. This neurotoxic piston attacks the nervous system and by way of comparison, it is in the same toxicity range as the venom of a cobra.

Although the man-of-war sting means instant death to small fish, the amount of poison carried in the stinging cells is rarely enough to be fatal to man.

Small fish paralyzed by the stinging cells are drawn up to the digestive apparatus by the contracting tentacles.

The man-of-war is a drifter at the mercy of wind and wave, with no control of direction or movement. It can be found in the Gulf Stream's warm waters from the Bahamas to Nova Scotia. It has been found in the Mediterranean and the Irish Sea; and from New Zealand to Southern California.

To a careless diver, the man-of-war means painful stings at best. The venom can induce anaphylaxis, an extreme, exaggerated physiologic reaction in which the victim's airway is constricted. As a consequence, the victim suffers extreme shortness of breath, coughing and wheezing. Intravenous injections of calcium gluconate have, in some cases, effectively relieved severe muscle cramp. At this time, unfortunately, there is still no foolproof antidote. In some rare instances, a man-of-war stinging has been fatal. Prevention lies in caution when diving in waters where this jellyfish abounds. Always scan the surface carefully when ascending.

STING RAY

Perhaps the most graceful creature in the sea, the sting ray actually seems to fly through the water with effortless sweeps of his wings. Although when full grown it may reach a length of eight feet, the sting ray is really a timid bottom-feeder. It prefers protected shallow areas like reefs and sheltered lagoons, where it can cruise the shallows until tired, then bury itself

Sting Ray

until nearly invisible to the diver's eye.

The poisonous stinger at the base of its muscular tail can be whipped back with great force if the sting ray is stepped on accidentally or purposely molested. The poison secreted by the stinger is virulent and can cause severe pain. Although this action is purely defensive, the stinger is large enough to inflict a serious wound.

Shuffling your swim fins when entering the water from a beach will frighten away any sting ray in the area. Be particularly careful when swimming close to the sandy bottom. If a diver is wounded in the chest or abdomen, the stinging could be fatal. Any sting ray wound should be treated by a doctor immediately.

The Octopus

OCTOPUS

No discussion of shy underwater creatures is complete without some mention of the bashful octopus. It is most active at night, preferring to remain safe inside its lair during the daylight hours.

The octopus has eight tentacles lined with powerful suckers which he uses to scramble across the bottom and to catch food. The catch, usually crab or lobster, is encircled by the tentacles and held securely by the suckers while the octopus tears away the meat with sharp pecks of a parrotlike beak set around its mouth. The bite of this beak is poisonous and the wise diver will confine his octopus activity to observation and photography. The bite of the octopus has been known to be fatal and indications are that the larger octopus *(the larger species may attain an armspread of 20 feet)* is considerably bolder than its more common little *(8 to 20 inches long)* brother.

The octopus is a swift swimmer; it jets itself through the water by drawing water into the muscular mantle that covers its body, then ejecting the water forcefully through a siphon.

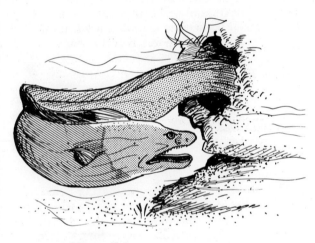

Moray Eel

MORAY EEL

At last count there were at least twenty recorded species of the moray family ranging from 18 inches to almost 12 feet in length. These species are to be found in tropical and sub-tropical waters the world over; however, it is the green moray *(common to waters of Florida, Bahamas, and the Caribbean)* which is most dangerous.

The green moray is a reef dweller by day and a slow swimming forager at night. A small coral reef may hide the nests of dozens of these eels. The moray has muscular jaws and strong teeth and becomes dangerous not because it is aggressive by disposition, but only when his lair is invaded.

This is of particular importance to divers gathering bugs *(langouste)* which also hide in coral crannies. The moray eel poses a serious threat to the diver who carelessly reaches into a dark crevice to pull a lobster. It can bite down with crushing force inflicting a jagged wound. It has been theorized that under such circumstances, the diver should stop struggling and the moray will soon release its hold.

Personally, I'd say the moray could probably outwait me. Divers in this situation have actually had to cut the moray's head off. Don't put your hand into a coral crevice unless you've carefully checked its tenants.

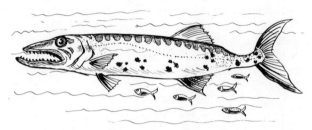

The Great Barracuda

GREAT BARRACUDA

The great barracuda can be a most awesome sight. It is sleek and torpedo-shaped, occasionally growing to a length of 10 feet and reaching a weight of 100 pounds. The barracuda has an unusual gill arrangement which enables it to swim with its mouth open, a somewhat disconcerting attribute from the novice diver's standpoint. The cuda's head makes up about 25 percent of its body length, and that head seems to be 90 percent filled with large fanglike teeth and rear grinders. These rear grinders do actually "grind" when the barracuda is irritated and this in turn produces an effect in the novice diver which is most interesting to observe.

This shallow water predator, an explosively fast swimmer, makes his home in Florida waters, the Bahamas, and throughout the Caribbean.

Although most Florida divers tend to disreguard it as an everpresent nuisance, the great barracuda has been known to attack man and cannot be completely ignored.

The presence of blood in the water will excite the barracuda, and it has been known to steal a speared fish before the diver can recover it. Divers are cautioned against wearing shiny medallions, watches, and the like; because in poor visibility the barracuda may mistake the flash of movement for a small fish. The barracuda is worthy of your respect and the wise diver will apply the same ground rules as mentioned for sharks. Generally speaking, the underwater photographer will find the barracuda to be quite timid, usually retreating as the diver advances.

Killer Whale

KILLER WHALE

The killer whale travels in fast moving "wolf packs," attacking and slaughtering herds of porpoise, seals, and sea lions, eating enormously to satisfy his voracious appetite.

The killer whale swims all the oceans, generally in schools of three to fifty, and is readily identified by its exceptionally high dorsal fin *(often six feet high)* and distinctive midnight black and white coloring.

The full-grown male may reach a body length of 30 feet. Some indication of their enormous food requirements might be gathered from the half-grown killer whale in whose stomach were found the partly-digested remains of 14 seals and 13 porpoises.

The killer whale, although no confirmed attacks of man have been recorded, must be regarded as a man eater. If a killer whale is sighted, leave the water immediately.

Myth or Maneater?

SHARK, MYTH OR MANEATER

When so much hatred and fear has been generated by fable, legend and myth, it is difficult to view the shark objectively.

There are about 250 species of shark, of which only a handful can be listed as so-called maneaters. Yet, the sight of a shark's dorsal fin cleaving the water will throw most people into absolute panic. The fact of the matter is that the chances of being struck by lightning *(approximately 1 million to one)* are far greater than being attacked by a shark.

No shark should be considered completely harmless and the most intelligent approach is to accord any shark, regardless of size or disposition, the same respect you would a strange dog. One well-known diver tells about meeting the undisputed lord of the sea, the great white shark. He describes watching in terror as the huge white raced up from the depths toward he and his diving companion, evidently unaware of their presence. When the shark finally sighted the divers, it became so terrified that it snapped around, emptied its bowels, and fled back to the depths. Incidentally, the largest of this family of confirmed maneaters ever captured, measured 21 feet and weighed more than 3½ tons!

NO AIR BLADDERS

Unlike bony fish which have air bladders to give them bouyancy, the cartiliginous shark has none and will sink if it stops swimming. And only by swimming will sufficient oxygen pass through its gills. As a result, the shark must swim from the moment of birth until death.

The shark is an undiscriminating scavenger prowling the surface of the sea constantly, hunting the crippled, the weak, and the old, taking whatever food comes its way. Sharks are attracted to their prey even when out of sight through their extraordinarily powerful sense of smell. A small amount of blood, traveling down-current from a speared fish, for example, may attract sharks from a mile away.

Sharks are also extremely sensitive to underwater sounds and vibrations. It has a most highly developed ability to locate the source of a sound, at far greater distances than it could possibly see them.

LATERAL LINE SENSORS

The shark has a long, fluid-filled canal running the length of both sides of its body. These *lateral* lines contain pressure sensors which are sensitive to low frequency vibrations. The normal swimming motions of fish or man generate rhythmic, low-frequency vibrations which will not excite the shark. However, erratic vibrations

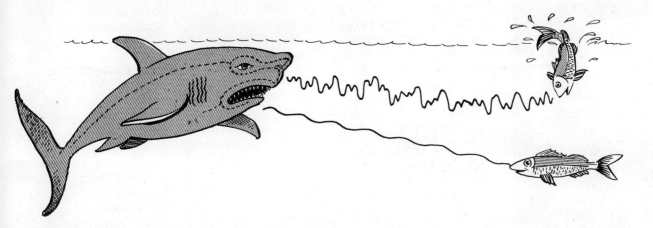

Lateral Line Sensors

made by a wounded fish, struggling on the end of a spear, will flash a message to the shark's brain and he will streak instinctively for the wounded fish.

On only one point do all shark authorities unanimously agree; the shark, any shark, is totally unpredictable.

There are increasing numbers of misinformed divers who believe the shark to be a timid, vastly overrated coward. The diver must never provoke a shark *(by spearing, riding, or tweaking his tail)* into attacking. There have been more authenticated shark bites attributed to the so-called "harmless" nurse shark than any other species. Blood attracts sharks. If you are cut by coral and bleeding, get out of the water. When spearfishing, toss your catch into the boat. Never carry speared fish on a stringer tied to your waist. Never dive in dirty water where underwater visibility is poor.

The shark has been driven off by yelling underwater, blowing bubbles at it, charging boldly, or even bouncing a camera housing off its nose. However, when a large shark is sighted, the wise diver swims slowly to his boat, keeping the shark in view until he is safely out of the water.

QUESTIONS ON CHAPTER 2

1. List several inanimate hazards of tropical diving and detail the preventative measures a diver can take to minimize these hazards.

2. Describe the proper procedure for diving in areas of strong tidal currents.

3. Explain a "rip" current. If caught in a "rip" current, what steps should the diver take?

4. What precautions would you take before diving in unfamiliar waters?

5. Explain the proper method for entering the water in heavy surf.

6. Describe the dangers of an encounter with the Portuguese man-of-war.

7. Why does the moray eel pose a particular threat to divers gathering lobster?

8. Explain the shark's sensitivity to the vibrations of a wounded fish.

9. In what way could a careless diver be injured by a stingray?

10. Describe the conditions which could precipitate aggressive shark behaviour.

"Can man go deeper? I feel he can. Equipment and techniques are now being investigated that should permit free-swimming aquanauts to explore and work on the ocean floor thousands of feet below the depths we can attain today."

Commander Scott Carpenter, U.S.N., *"Look Magazine"*

Chapter 3   UNDERWATER PHYSICS

Any good diver will tell you that safety and knowledge are directly proportional. In other words, the more you learn about diving, the more confident and safe a diver you'll become.

The sport diver is not expected to be a master physicist, but a good grasp of the fundamentals of underwater physics will go a long way toward clarifying the limitations imposed by the environment on man and equipment.

Anyone who would strap on a diving-lung without completely understanding these limitations can only succeed in bringing painful if not disastrous results upon himself.

The differences between our usual land-locked environment and the sea are monumental. If one were to select the greatest difference between the two, it would have to be pressure.

For example, because of its great density, water pressure increases about ½ pound per square inch for every foot of depth. Pressure is ordinarily measured in pounds per square inch (*p.s.i.*). Man's deepest recorded dive is 2,000 feet where the total pressure is approximately 1,000 p.s.i. The total weight on the diver at that depth is equivalent to 1,250 tons!

Virtually any physiological change that may occur underwater is a result of the direct or indirect effects of pressure.

Underwater Physics

ATMOSPHERIC PRESSURE

The earth is surrounded by a gaseous envelope called the atmosphere. This envelope of air exerts a pressure equal to the total weight of the miles of air in the atmosphere. It exerts a measurable weight at sea level of 14.7 pounds on each square inch of the earth's surface.

Imagine a column of air rising above one square inch at sea level and extending to the uppermost part of the atmosphere. It would weigh 14.7 pounds.

As a result, the term "one atmosphere" is used to denote a pressure of 14.7 p.s.i. A total pres-

The pressure of the air against this one square inch of white surface is 14.7 lbs.

Atmospheric Pressure

GAGE PRESSURE

When pressures are to be measured, gauges which have been corrected to read zero at sea level are used to indicate the pressure differential between the pressure being measured and the surrounding pressure.

For example, depth gauges worn on a diver's wrist are calibrated to read zero pressure at sea level. By calibrating this gauge in feet of depth, relatively accurate readings may be taken at any depth.

Pressure readings taken on a fully charged diving cylinder usually read 2,250 p.s.i. which means in effect that the cylinder pressure is 2,250 p.s.i. above atmospheric pressure.

Pressure thus obtained is called "GAGE PRESSURE" and designated as pounds per square inch, gage (p.s.i.g.).

ABSOLUTE PRESSURE

Absolute or ambient pressure is the true pressure on a diver at any depth and is the sum of the gage pressure and the atmospheric pressure.

To convert gage pressure to absolute pressure, atmospheric pressure must be added.

In calculating diving problems, absolute pressure must be used in all gas law equations.

Absolute pressure is designated as pounds per square inch absolute *(p.s.i.a.)*.

Underwater physics may be defined as a science dealing with the natural forces acting upon the diver underwater; these forces being the result of the properties and behavior of matter.

sure of 147 p.s.i. would be expressed as "ten atmospheres."

The average man has about 2,500 square inches of body area. As a result of the atmospheric pressure, at sea level he is subjected to almost 19 tons of pressure!

Having been born to it, plus the fact that the air we breathe is of equal pressure, we rarely think about the existence of atmospheric pressure.

AMBIENT PRESSURE	
HEIGHT ABOVE AND DEPTH BELOW SEA LEVEL	PRESSURE PER SQUARE INCH
53,907 Ft.	1.47 p.s.i.
38,389 Ft.	2.54 p.s.i.
17,962 Ft.	7.35 p.s.i.
SEA LEVEL	14.7 p.s.i.
33 Ft.	29.4 p.s.i.
66 Ft.	44.1 p.s.i.
99 Ft.	58.8 p.s.i.

Ambient Pressure Chart

As indicated above, the pressure exerted by the atmosphere decreases with higher elevations.

For example, at an elevation of 18,000 feet the pressure exerted by the atmosphere is roughly 7.35 p.s.i. or half the atmospheric pressure *(14.7 p.s.i.)* measured at sea level.

MATTER

Matter has been described as anything which occupies space and has weight. There are three states of matter:

SOLIDS - which have a definite volume and shape

LIQUIDS - which have a definite volume and weight but take the shape of their containers, and are considered incompressible.

GASES - which have neither a definite volume nor shape but are compressible.

Although the diver's equipment consists of solids, he is principally concerned with the other two states of matter: LIQUIDS (the water in which he swims) and, GASES (the air he breathes).

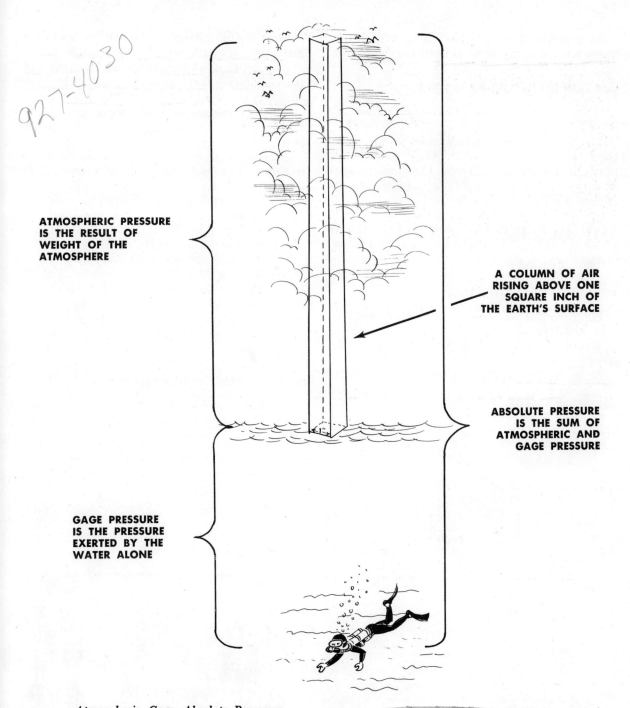

ATMOSPHERIC PRESSURE
IS THE RESULT OF
WEIGHT OF THE
ATMOSPHERE

A COLUMN OF AIR
RISING ABOVE ONE
SQUARE INCH OF
THE EARTH'S SURFACE

ABSOLUTE PRESSURE
IS THE SUM OF
ATMOSPHERIC AND
GAGE PRESSURE

GAGE PRESSURE
IS THE PRESSURE
EXERTED BY THE
WATER ALONE

Atmospheric, Gage, Absolute Pressures

WATER

WATER IS DENSE

Dive to the bottom of a swimming pool and you will feel an increasing pressure on your ears. It is immediately apparent that water exerts pressure.

This water pressure is a result of its weight, or more properly its density. The density then of water is really the weight of a specified volume *(cubic foot)* of water. Because water is much more dense than air, the pressure underwater climbs quickly with increasing depth. The weight of one cubic foot of fresh water is 62.4 pounds.

15

As a result of its dissolved salts, average sea water has a density of 64 pounds per cubic foot.

WATER IS INCOMPRESSIBLE

Since water is virtually incompressible, its density remains the same regardless of depth.

The pressure produced by water is the direct result of its weight, and therefore increases in direct proportion to its depth. The gage pressure at a depth of 100 feet will be doubled that of 50 feet.

As a result, the pressure on a diver at any depth is equal to the sum weight of the feet of water above him. This water pressure surrounding the diver is exerted equally in all directions.

PRESSURE CALCULATION

For practical purposes, it may be considered that water pressure increases by one pound per square inch for each two foot increment of descent.

Actually, the pressure exerted per foot of depth in sea water is *0.445 p.s.i.* and *0.432 p.s.i.* per foot of fresh water.

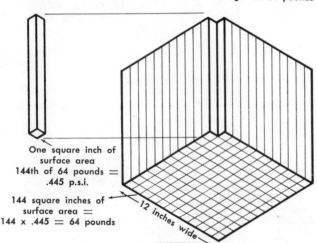

Weight = 64 pounds

One square inch of surface area 144th of 64 pounds = .445 p.s.i.

144 square inches of surface area = 144 x .445 = 64 pounds

12 inches wide

Consider a Cubic Foot of Sea Water

Consider a cubic foot of sea water! It weighs 64 pounds and measures 12 inches (height) by 12 inches (width) by 12 inches (depth). Its total weight (64 pounds) presses down on one square foot of surface area (bottom). Since there are 144 square inches in a square foot, the pressure on each square inch is 64 pounds divided by 144 square inches or 0.445 pounds per square inch.

Multiplying the feet of depth by 0.445 p.s.i. gives the gage pressure at that depth in p.s.i.

At a depth of 33 feet, the diver has added 14.7 pounds of water pressure per square inch of body surface. *(33 x 0.445 p.s.i. = 14.7 p.s.i.g.)*.

This is the equivalent of atmospheric pressure and is expressed as one atmosphere of gage pressure.

This pressure continues to mount by one atmosphere *(14.7 p.s.i.)* for each additional 33 foot increment of depth.

However, we have been discussing only water *(gage)* pressure. As you know, the diver must add the atmospheric pressure to determine the absolute pressure at depth.

For example, the absolute pressure at 33 feet in sea water is 29.4 p.s.i. *(2 atmospheres of pressure)* which is double the surface pressure.

Not until 99 feet will the absolute pressure double again *(58.8 p.s.i. or 4 atmospheres)*.

The pressure will not double again until 231 feet *(8 atmospheres)* is reached.

WATER HAS BUOYANCY

If while treading water the student diver takes a deep breath and holds it, he finds that he floats

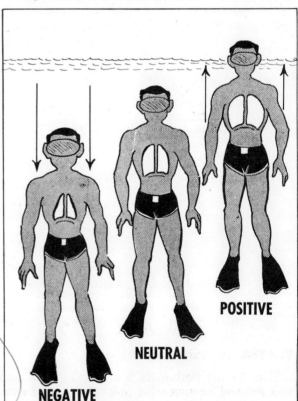

POSITIVE

NEUTRAL

NEGATIVE

Water Has Buoyancy

effortlessly. However, releasing his breath will send him slowly sinking.

This effect is a result of his lung capacity. When the lungs are inflated they will support the diver like an inflated life vest.

Although lung capacity varies with individuals, everyone will be buoyed up when the lungs are inflated.

Let's consider a diver of average size. He weighs 184 pounds. By immersing him in a brimming tank and weighing the run-off water, we can calculate that the buoyant force supporting the diver exactly equals the weight of the displaced water.

In this case the diver has displaced 3 cubic feet of sea water and is positively buoyant.

ARCHIMEDES' PRINCIPLE

"Any object wholly or partially immersed in a liquid is buoyed up by a force equal to the weight of the liquid displaced."

As indicated by Archimedes' principle, since our diver displaces 3 cubic feet of water, he is buoyed up by a force of 192 pounds *(3 c.f. x 64 lbs./ft³ = 192)*. Subtracting the diver's weight *(184 pounds)* leaves him positively buoyant by eight pounds. To obtain neutral buoyancy, eight pounds must be added to his weight belt. Any more weight would make him negatively buoyant.

The specific gravity of a substance is its density compared with that of water, which is arbitrarily fixed at 1.0.

For example, the specific gravity of aluminum is 2.72 which means that it weighs 2.72 times the weight of an equal volume of water or that it is 2.72 times as dense as water.

As a result any object whose density *(specific gravity)* is less than that of water will float, while one whose density is greater will sink.

Since the diver's body is largely water (over 65%), it has a density almost equal to that of water.

If a cubic foot of average sea water weighs 64 pounds and a cubic foot of styrofoam weighs only one half pound — it is obvious that the styrofoam cannot displace a cubic foot of water which is far heavier, and therefore will float.

In order that the diver swim comfortably underwater, he must maintain a balance between negative and positive buoyancy. This state of balance is called neutral buoyancy.

Underwater Sound

WATER TRANSMITS SOUND

The many poetic references to its silence, notwithstanding, the underwater world can be a very noisy place.

The metallic tinkle of exhaust bubbles escaping from his regulator is as reassuring to a diver as his heartbeat. Underwater sounds are made by marine life as well as the movements of the water. Shipwrecks can make the most horrendous sounds as they creak and groan under the movement of water about them.

Displacement Equals Buoyancy

Sound travels at about 4,800 feet per second through water. In air sound travels at only 1,090 feet per second.

Despite the fact that sound travels four times as fast in water, voice communications are all but impossible. The most successful underwater language is one of hand signals which though somewhat limited usually produces good results.

Even sounds originating at the surface are almost impossible to hear. Only one part of sound energy in 10,000ths will penetrate the water.

To attract the attention of a buddy some distance away, rap against the air tank with a knife or stone. This produces a clear sharp sound which can be easily heard. Unfortunately, the direction of underwater sounds is most difficult to determine.

On shore, a blindfolded man can localize to within 10 degrees of a sound's source.

Underwater, due to the much higher speed of sound, direction finding by sound is practically impossible.

WATER CONDUCTS HEAT

Normal body temperature is considered to be 98.6°F. Anytime his unprotected body is exposed to cold water, the diver loses heat into the water around him by direct conduction through his skin.

Water has a high degree of heat conduction in contrast to air which is a poor conductor. In water less than 70°F., the temperature difference between the water and normal body temperature (98.6°F.) will cause heat to be lost from the body faster than it can be produced. As the water gets progressively colder, the body burns more oxygen to try to offset heat loss. If body heat is not quickly restored, chilling and loss of function will soon follow.

Usually, temperature tends to drop as we move progressively higher; for example, climbing mountains, flying planes. This decrease in temperature is a steady and calculable figure. Quite the opposite is true in diving. The temperature underwater may drop drastically, suddenly and distinctly. This phenomenon is called a thermocline.

It is necessary when diving in cold water that the diver wear a protective exposure suit.

Exposure suits restrict heat conduction by insulating the body from the water.

The denser water of the thermocline may be so pronounced that a diver carrying slightly negative bouyancy will sink through the warmer,

NORMAL BODY TEMPERATURE — 98.6

— 90°F

— 80°F · NO SUIT REQUIRED

— 70°F

— 60°F · WET SUIT REQUIRED

— 50°F

— 40°F · DRY SUIT RECOMMENDED

FREEZING POINT OF WATER

— 30°F

Water Conducts Heat

less dense water and settle at the top of the thermocline. Midwest divers operating in the thermocline periodically swim up into the warmer water to slow down body heat loss. Exposure suits are an absolute must when swimming below the thermocline.

WATER DISTORTS VISION AND LIGHT

In this strange environment, things we have always taken for granted on shore take on new and special significance.

Sight underwater is impossible without introducing an air space between the eye and water. Hence, the mask.

Because of this air space, however, objects appear to be one third (1/3) larger than their actual size. Conversely, distances underwater are misjudged to be 25% closer than their actual distance.

This effect is known as REFRACTION and is the result of the bending of light rays as they pass from the dense water into the air space within the mask.

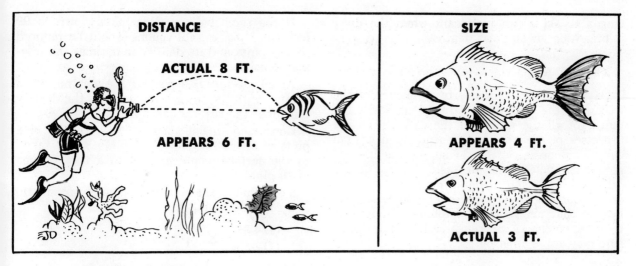

DISTANCE

ACTUAL 8 FT.

APPEARS 6 FT.

SIZE

APPEARS 4 FT.

ACTUAL 3 FT.

Water Distorts Vision

This bending gives a false impression of size and position of underwater objects. For example, the fish in the illustration is actually 8 feet away, but refraction makes it appear 6 feet. The diver makes adjustments to depth and size perception quickly with experience.

Visibility

Divers tend to describe diving conditions in terms of underwater visibility, the maximum lateral distance over which an object can still be seen.

Visibility underwater depends on many factors. If the water is turbid or dirty, the diver's vision will be obscured. However, water often stratifys into alternate layers of clear and turbid water.

When the water's surface is rough and choppy, much light is reflected and never enters the water. A high percentage of the sun's rays are also absorbed and warm the surface water. The wise underwater photographer waits for high noon since the brighter and the higher the sun, the greater the penetration of light.

Diffusion

Particles of silt or plankton suspended in water tend to deflect and distort the light rays. This effect is so pronounced that even in crystal water 75% of the light rays are diffused in the first 16 feet of water depth.

Absorption

Sunlight is a composite of all colors and water filters the colors with increasing depth. As light penetrates the water, the reds are absorbed quickly, and oranges last only a few feet deeper. Yellows filter out at approximately 32 feet, leaving only greens, blues and finally black. Almost all color, except blue, will be scrubbed below 60 feet.

AIR

AIR IS A MIXTURE

Although we speak of air as though it were a single gas, it is really a mixture of gases.

Like all mixtures, the composition of air is not absolutely uniform, and may vary in composition and water vapor content with different altitudes and weather conditions.

SUBSTANCE	PERCENT BY VOLUME
NITROGEN	77.14
OXYGEN	20.69
RARE GASES	0.93
CARBON DIOXIDE	0.03
WATER VAPOR	1.20

Composition of Air Chart

NITROGEN (N_2)

Nitrogen constitutes the largest part of air. Although incapable of supporting life by itself, its presence is essential to the life processes. It is colorless, odorless and tasteless. It is at least five times as soluble in fatty tissue as it is in water. It is this characteristic, that causes nitrogen to act as an intoxicant when the diver is breathing air at great depths.

OXYGEN (O₂)

Oxygen accounts for nearly a quarter of the weight of the atmosphere around us and eight tenths of all the waters of the earth. The life processes of every animal depend upon oxygen since it alone is capable of supporting life. It is without color, odor or taste *(except under high pressure where it has a definite taste described both as sweet and sour)* and is slightly heavier than air, volume for volume. Under certain circumstances, oxygen breathed under pressure may act as a poison.

CARBON DIOXIDE (CO₂)

CO₂ is always present in air. Normally, there are about three parts of carbon dioxide in ten thousand parts of air. *(0.03 percent)*. This proportion may double or triple in a crowded room due to the exhalations of people. The gas is colorless, odorless and tasteless in ordinary concentrations. When present in increased amounts it has both an acidic taste and odor due to the formation of carbonic acid when the CO₂ combines with moisture inside the mouth. CO₂ is generated in the body tissues, the waste product of the metabolic processes of the body cells.

High concentrations of CO₂ in a diver's breathing air can produce most harmful effects.

AIR IS COMPRESSIBLE

"The *volume* of a gas varies *inversely* as the *absolute pressure* while the *density* varies *directly* as the *absolute pressure*, provided the temperature is constant." BOYLE'S LAW

The more a gas is compressed, the smaller its volume will become. If the pressure is doubled, the gas will occupy half its original volume. Triple the pressure and volume will be cut to one third. Meanwhile, the density is doubled and tripled respectively.

The importance of this law to the diver lies in understanding the volume changes of gases resulting from depth-pressures.

As depth-pressure increases, the volume of a gas becomes proportionally smaller.

For example, if a balloon containing 10 pints of air at the surface is taken down to 33 feet in seawater *(29.4 p.s.i.a.)*, its volume will be compressed to 5 pints while its density is doubled.

If the same balloon were taken down to 99 feet *(58.8 p.s.i.a.)* its volume would be reduced to 2½ pints and its density four times the original density.

At 297 feet *(147.0 p.s.i.a.)* the volume would be one tenth the surface volume, and the density ten times the surface density.

Conversely, a balloon filled to a volume of 2 pints of air at 132 feet *(73.5 p.s.i.a.)* and taken to the surface would expand to a new volume of 10 pints.

To calculate the volume change at any depth, use the following formula:

$$\frac{(D+33)}{(D+33)} \times V_1 = V_2$$

NOTE: On *descent*, the volume (V_2) must get smaller. Place the greater depth (D) on bottom of equation in the divisor.

On *ascent*, the volume (V_2) must get larger. Place the greater depth (D) on top of equation in the dividend.

SAMPLE PROBLEM: Determine the volume (V_2) of a balloon filled with 10 pints of air at a depth of 165 feet in sea water — and taken up to the surface.

$$\frac{165 + 33}{0 + 33} \times 10 \text{ pints} = V_2$$

$$\frac{198}{33} = 6 \text{ Atmos. } \times 10 \text{ pints} = 60 \text{ pints}$$

AIR IS EXPANDABLE

"The volume of a gas varies directly as its absolute temperature, if the pressure remains constant." CHARLES' LAW.

If the absolute temperature of a balloon filled with 10 pints of air at 14.7 p.s.i. were doubled, the balloon would expand to twice its original volume.

However, if the volume were to remain constant *(a high pressure cylinder, for example)* while the absolute temperature was doubled, the pressure would correspondingly double.

Normally this is not an important consideration. Should a fully-charged cylinder undergo a great temperature increase however, *(as in a fire or exposed to excessively hot sun rays)* the cylinder might exceed its safe pressure limitations and blow off through the safety plug in the cylinder valve.

DEPTH SEA WATER	ABSOLUTE ATMOS.	PRESSURE LBS./SQ.IN.	VOLUME INCREASE ON ASCENT	VOLUME DECREASE ON DESCENT	DENSITY	DEPTH FRESH WATER
0'	1	14.7	100 PINTS		SURFACE DENSITY	0'
33'	2	29.4	50 PINTS	1/2 ORIGINAL VOLUME	2 X SURFACE DENSITY	34'
66'	3	44.0	33.3 PINTS	1/3 ORIGINAL VOLUME	3 X SURFACE DENSITY	68'
99'	4	58.8	25 PINTS	1/4 ORIGINAL VOLUME	4 X SURFACE DENSITY	102'
132'	5	73.5	20 PINTS	1/5 ORIGINAL VOLUME	5 X SURFACE DENSITY	136'
165'	6	88.2	16.6 PINTS	1/6 ORIGINAL VOLUME	6 X SURFACE DENSITY	170'
198'	7	102.9	14.2 PINTS	1/7 ORIGINAL VOLUME	7 X SURFACE DENSITY	204'
231'	8	117.6	12.5 PINTS	1/8 ORIGINAL VOLUME	8 X SURFACE DENSITY	238'
264'	9	132.3	11.1 PINTS	1/9 ORIGINAL VOLUME	9 X SURFACE DENSITY	272'
297'	10	147.0	10 PINTS	1/10 ORIGINAL VOLUME	10 X SURFACE DENSITY	306'

Boyle's Law Chart

AIR COMPONENTS EXERT INDEPENDENT PRESSURES

As we have already learned, air is not a single gas but rather a mixture of gases. Each gas in this mixture exerts an independent share of the total pressure.

"The partial pressure of each gas in a mixture is proportional to the relative amount *(by volume)* of that gas in the mixture." DALTON'S LAW

Fill a 1 pint container with oxygen at atmospheric pressure. *(14.7 p.s.i.)*

Now, if a pint of nitrogen at atmospheric pressure is forced into the same container, 2 pints of gas have been compressed into a volume of 1 pint.

Assuming the temperature remains unchanged, the total pressure of the mixture of the 2 gases will double. *(29.4 p.s.i.).*

Each gas in the mixture exerts the same pressure as it did before the mixture was made. The pressure each gas exerts is its *partial pressure.*

At sea level, nitrogen exerts approximately 80% of the atmospheric pressure, *(14.7 p.s.i. x*

21

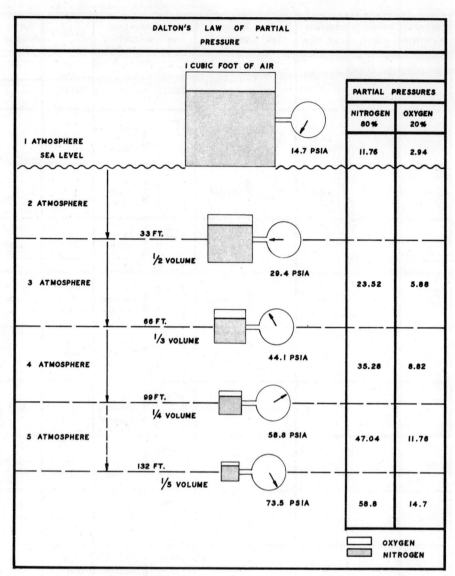

DALTON'S LAW OF PARTIAL PRESSURE

I CUBIC FOOT OF AIR

	PARTIAL PRESSURES	
	NITROGEN 80%	OXYGEN 20%
I ATMOSPHERE SEA LEVEL — 14.7 PSIA	11.76	2.94
2 ATMOSPHERE — 33 FT. ½ VOLUME — 29.4 PSIA		
3 ATMOSPHERE	23.52	5.88
66 FT. ⅓ VOLUME — 44.1 PSIA		
4 ATMOSPHERE	35.28	8.82
99 FT. ¼ VOLUME — 58.8 PSIA		
5 ATMOSPHERE	47.04	11.76
132 FT. ⅕ VOLUME — 73.5 PSIA	58.8	14.7

☐ OXYGEN
▨ NITROGEN

Dalton's Law Chart

.80 = 11.7 p.s.i.) and oxygen approximately 20% (14.7 p.s.i. x .20 = 2.94 p.s.i.).

At a depth of 132 feet, the partial pressure of oxygen will increase to 14.7 p.s.i.a. and nitrogen to 58.8 p.s.i.a.

Note the proportion of approximately 4:1 has been maintained. The mathematical determinations are:

Partial pressure of Oxygen [(132 x .445) + 14.7] x .20 = 14.7 p.s.i.a.

Partial pressure of Nitrogen [(132 x .445) + 14.7] x .80 = 58.8 p.s.i.a.

If at sea level, the partial pressure of nitrogen in the body is 11.7 p.s.i., at 132 feet *(5 atmospheres)* its partial pressure will increase to 58.8 p.s.i.a. indicating that five times as much

nitrogen will be contained in the body solely as the result of increased pressure.

Although gas partial pressures are relatively unimportant at shallow depths, they become particularly significant as the total pressure increases with depth.

AIR IS SOLUBLE

"At a constant temperature, the solubility of any gas in a liquid is almost directly proportional to the pressure the gas exerts on the liquid." HENRY'S LAW

If a mixture of gases is bubbled through a liquid, the solubility of each gas is proportional to its partial pressure. Each gas dissolves to the same degree as it would *(at the same pressure)* if the other gases were not present.

As the partial pressure of a gas increases, the amount of the gas that will go into solution in the liquid increases. Conversely, as the partial pressure is reduced, the amount held in solution will decrease.

When the amount of gas dissolved in a liquid equals the partial pressure of that gas, the liquid is said to be saturated and is capable of holding no more at that depth-pressure.

It is this important aspect of the Law of Solubility that permitted the development of an operational saturation diving system which will be covered fully in the chapter, *"BUBBLE TROUBLE."*

Note:

The student-diver may become understandably up-tight about being expected to commit the gas laws to memory. However, the following memory jogger may help in remembering:

Better	— B —	Boyle's Law
Ventilated	— V —	Volume
Drawers	— D —	Dalton's Law
Pamper	— P —	Partial
Peoples	— P —	Pressures
Hind	— H —	Henry's
Sides	— S —	Solubility

AVAILABLE AIR CHART

EFFECT OF TOTAL PRESSURE
Actual Contents · Ambient Pressure · Regulator-Lung System

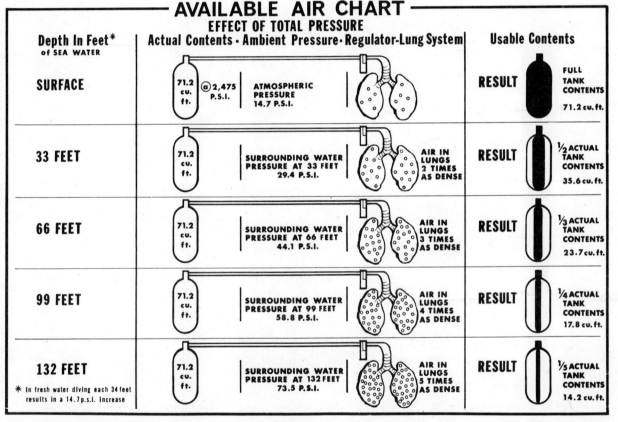

Depth In Feet* of SEA WATER	Actual Contents · Ambient Pressure · Regulator-Lung System	Usable Contents
SURFACE	71.2 cu. ft. @ 2,475 P.S.I. ATMOSPHERIC PRESSURE 14.7 P.S.I.	RESULT — FULL TANK CONTENTS 71.2 cu. ft.
33 FEET	71.2 cu. ft. SURROUNDING WATER PRESSURE AT 33 FEET 29.4 P.S.I. AIR IN LUNGS 2 TIMES AS DENSE	RESULT — ½ ACTUAL TANK CONTENTS 35.6 cu. ft.
66 FEET	71.2 cu. ft. SURROUNDING WATER PRESSURE AT 66 FEET 44.1 P.S.I. AIR IN LUNGS 3 TIMES AS DENSE	RESULT — ⅓ ACTUAL TANK CONTENTS 23.7 cu. ft.
99 FEET	71.2 cu. ft. SURROUNDING WATER PRESSURE AT 99 FEET 58.8 P.S.I. AIR IN LUNGS 4 TIMES AS DENSE	RESULT — ¼ ACTUAL TANK CONTENTS 17.8 cu. ft.
132 FEET	71.2 cu. ft. SURROUNDING WATER PRESSURE AT 132 FEET 73.5 P.S.I. AIR IN LUNGS 5 TIMES AS DENSE	RESULT — ⅕ ACTUAL TANK CONTENTS 14.2 cu. ft.

* In fresh water diving each 34 feet results in a 14.7 p.s.i. increase

As explained earlier, the diver must breathe air at a pressure equal to that of the surrounding water. The regulator-lung system accomplishes this nicely, however, at the sacrifice of usable contents. The Available Air Chart above illustrates the relationship between the incompressable tank and the air available to the diver (results of Boyle's Law). As high pressure air is released from the tank it is reduced in proportion to the pressure of the surrounding water. As a result, the reduction in usable (available) air is directly related to the absolute pressure. Regardless of the depth-pressure, the lungs require a constant volume of air. However, since gas density increases proportionately with increasing absolute pressure (depth), a correspondingly greater density of air is required to fill the lungs to the same volume. The Chart further illustrates the relationship between original volume and available air. For example: At a depth of 66 feet, the amount of usable air would be 1/3 the rated volume of the tank. This is equivalent to the volume of a smaller tank (23.7 cubic ft.) at atmospheric pressure.

QUESTIONS ON CHAPTER 3

1. What are the major components of air and their percentages?

2. What is meant by: a) Atmospheric pressure b) Gage pressure c) Absolute pressure?

3. What is the weight of one cubic foot of: a) Sea Water b) Fresh Water?

4. What is the gage pressure at a depth of 69 feet in sea water?

5. If a diver is at a depth of 34 feet in fresh water, how much deeper must he descend to double the pressure on his body?

6. What is the absolute pressure at a depth of 135 feet in fresh water?

7. If a balloon contained 10 pints of air at the surface, what would its volume be at a depth of 96 feet in sea water?

8. Define the term "Thermocline".

9. Calculate the partial pressure of nitrogen in air at a depth of 176 feet in sea water.

10. A camera housing has a volume of 0.25 cubic feet and weighs 3 pounds. A 12 pound camera and a light meter weighing ½ pound are to be mounted inside the housing. Since the camera is to be used in sea water, how much weight (if any) is required for neutral buoyancy?

> *"The diver is fascinated by the exploration of the depths of the ocean; the physiologist has always been interested to know the limits of performance of the human body."*
>
> Doctor Albert Buhlmann, *"The Undersea Challenge"*

Chapter 4   UNDERWATER PHYSIOLOGY

The diver enters a foreign environment where even the act of breathing, the most automatic human function, may require conscious effort. The air he breathes may be 5 times as "thick" as normal atmospheric air, and muscular effort is required just to breathe.

He enters a strange and silent world, where natural light is subdued and sounds are muted and distant.

And he also knows he is the intruder and is only allowed to remain until his breathing supply is exhausted. Then, he must retrace his steps to the surface.

If he is to dive safely, the diver's knowledge must extend beyond physical law. To establish his own limits the diver must understand the elemental forces which act upon his body. He must understand the basic structure of the body and the function of its vital organs. And knowing this — he will understand the effects of increased pressure on the human anatomy. Underwater physiology is the science of the orderly and disorderly function of the body in a marine environment.

ANATOMY OF A DIVER

For the most part, the human body is composed of fluids through which pressure is freely transmitted and solids that are practically incompressible. The body fluids are blood, tissue fluids, and fluid in body cells. The solids are those body components which are relatively incompressible *(non-air containing)* including the bones, muscles, heart and liver.

Since his body is virtually incompressible, it would seem the diver needn't concern himself about pressure.

Unfortunately, a small portion of the body consists of natural air-containing spaces and since air is compressible and greatly affected by pressure changes, certain problems can occur and are therefore of special interest to the diver. These natural air spaces are the middle ear and eustachian tube, sinuses, stomach and intestine *(although these do not normally contain air)*, the lungs and associated airways.

THE LUNGS

Get rid of the idea that the lungs are just two big balloons in the center of the chest. They aren't.

A cross section of a human lung would closely resemble a sponge with the millions of little air sacs representing the lung alveoli.

Man has two major body cavities. The upper cavity is called the thorax and is partitioned by the muscular diaphragm from the lower *(abdominal)* cavity. The lungs are contained within the thorax and are separated from each other by a space in the center of the chest called the mediastinum which also contains the heart.

The lungs have been further described as an upside-down hollow tree. The tree trunk represents the *trachea*, which branches right and left into the *bronchial tubes*. These again branch into numerous twigs covered by thousands of leaves *(alveoli)*. The membrane which covers the lung surface is called the *pleura*.

RESPIRATION

Respiration is simply the act of breathing. With each breath a volume of air flows into the lungs and is then expelled. The whole respiratory system serves only to bring fresh air into

25

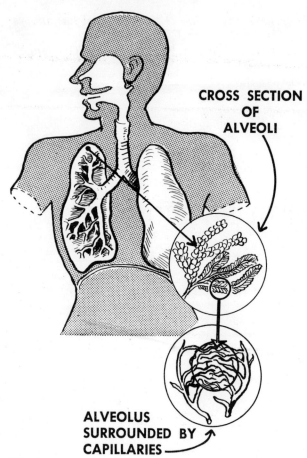

CROSS SECTION OF ALVEOLI

ALVEOLUS SURROUNDED BY CAPILLARIES

The Lungs

sugar into a compartmented container of water. Its molecules will diffuse throughout the compartment and then — through the permeable membrane into the next compartment. This diffusion will continue until an equilibrium is established and the molecules are evenly dispersed on both sides of the permeable membrane.

In the human lungs, the permeable membrane is the one cell thick alveolar wall and gas molecules exchange as freely through it as the sugar molecules pass through the permeable membrane in the illustration.

As the blood circulates, it carries oxygen to all the body cells combining with food substances containing carbon to produce energy, warmth, and carbon dioxide. This process is known as *metabolism*.

Respiration consists essentially of two separate but interdependent functions: EXTERNAL RESPIRATION AND INTERNAL RESPIRATION.

EXTERNAL RESPIRATION

The diaphragm is normally arched upward in the relaxed position. When this muscle descends, the chest cavity is enlarged, lowering the air pressure inside. This is an automatic action requiring no conscious effort.

Air rushes into the lungs inflating the thousands of alveoli, the lungs increasing in size as much as the expanded chest permits.

When the diaphragm is relaxed, the lungs contract and force the air out the same airways. It is no longer the same air, for it has transferred

the lungs to supply oxygen and remove carbon dioxide from the blood.

The thin wall of each alveoli contains tiny blood vessels called *capillaries*. Millions of these capillaries surround the alveoli to make up the lung capillary bed. True respiration only takes place in the alveoli. Oxygen from the air is brought into close contact with the lung capillary bed and enters the blood. At the same time, carbon dioxide transfers from the blood into the air.

DIFFUSION

Understanding the manner in which gas molecules pass in and out of cells will help immeasurably in understanding not only the complexities of respiration but also many of the diving maladies. All molecules are in a state of constant movement. Gas molecules are particularly free, being restricted only by the containing vessel. Diffusion has been defined as "breaking out of concentration". For example, drop a lump of

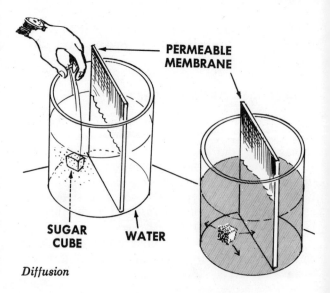

PERMEABLE MEMBRANE

SUGAR CUBE   WATER

Diffusion

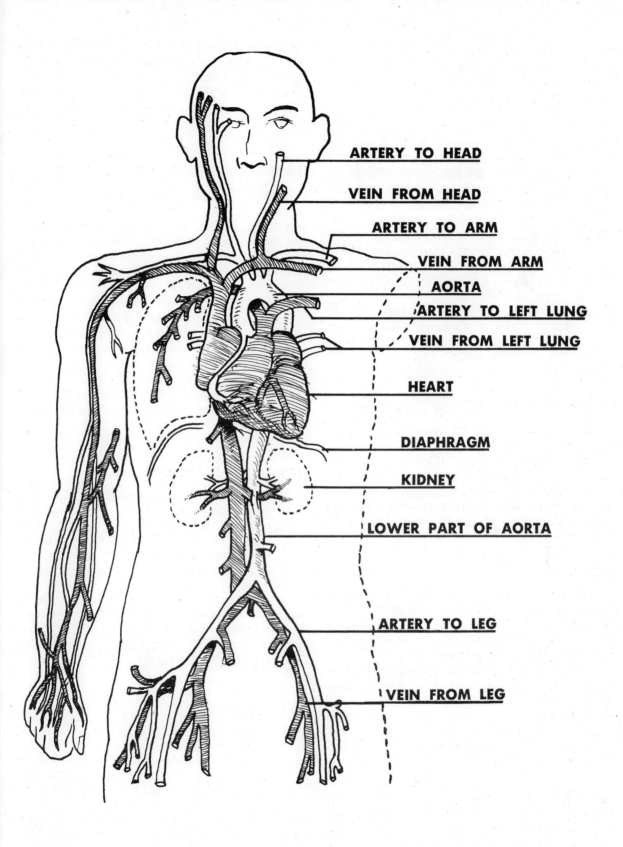

ARTERY TO HEAD

VEIN FROM HEAD

ARTERY TO ARM

VEIN FROM ARM

AORTA

ARTERY TO LEFT LUNG

VEIN FROM LEFT LUNG

HEART

DIAPHRAGM

KIDNEY

LOWER PART OF AORTA

ARTERY TO LEG

VEIN FROM LEG

The Circulatory System

oxygen to the blood and taken up carbon dioxide to be exhaled into the outside air.

INTERNAL RESPIRATION

In the alveoli, oxygen molecules diffuse into the capillary blood. The hemoglobin in the red blood cells picks up the oxygen and transports it to the tissues. At the same time, carbon dioxide is returned to the lungs primarily in solution in the plasma and diffused out of the blood into the alveoli.

The lungs expand and contract with a regular rhythm. At rest, the average man breathes about 16 times per minute. He takes in about one pint of air at each breath; this is called *tidal air*. The average lungs, expanded by the deepest inhalation, will hold approximately 10 pints of air. Even after the most forceful of exhalations, a given amount of air will remain in the lungs, usually two to three pints. This is called *residual volume*.

HEART AND CIRCULATORY SYSTEM

For every day of his life, the average man's heart will beat a hundred thousand times, circulating the five or six quarts of blood in his body constantly. This blood, incidentally, accounts for about a fifteenth of his total weight. In a single day the heart will contract 100,000 times to pump 4,300 gallons of blood through the body's circulatory system!

BLOOD

The blood is composed of liquids and solids. The liquid portion, plasma, is 90% water which enables the blood to flow easily in the circulatory system. The solids consist mainly of red and white blood cells and platelets.

In the red blood cell is an iron-containing substance called *hemoglobin* which has the ability to combine with oxygen in the lungs and carry it to the body tissue. It is also the hemoglobin which gives blood the red color. The oxygenated blood turns scarlet, while blood carrying carbon dioxide is generally dark red.

HEART

The heart is a muscular organ which functions as a double pump. It is divided into four chambers: the (2) *auricles*, which receive the blood and; the (2) *ventricles*, which have thick muscular walls in order to pump the blood through the body. Through these four chambers the heart circulates the blood simultaneously through two circulatory systems: the *greater circulation* and the *lesser circulation*.

GREATER CIRCULATION

Freshly oxygenated blood is carried from the lungs to the left auricle where it is pumped to the left ventricle. From here it is pumped into the large *artery*, the *aorta*. Arteries are thick-walled, muscular blood vessels which carry blood away from the heart to all parts of the body. These arteries become progressively smaller until they empty into tiny *capillaries*.

These tiny blood vessels are made up of one layer cells, and through this thin wall food and oxygen diffuse out of the blood into the tissue cells.

At the same time, carbon dioxide enters the blood and is passed on into larger and larger *veins*, which carry the blood to the right auricle of the heart.

LESSER CIRCULATION

The right auricle contracts, sending the blood into the right ventricle. From here the blood is pumped into an artery, forking right and left, carrying the blood to the right and left lungs.

In the lungs, the blood gives up carbon dioxide and takes up a fresh supply of oxygen from the inspired air.

Veins return the oxygenated blood to the left auricle to be pumped into the greater circulation.

The interruption of either system has serious implications. Body cells cannot live very long without this oxygen supply.

THE SINUSES

"The function of the sinuses is not definitely known. Various theories give them the same function as the *nasal cavities, (warming, moistening, and filtering the air; aiding in resonance, and making the skull lighter).*" Taber's Cyclopedic Medical Dictionary.

The paranasal sinuses are air-containing spaces located in the bones of the face and skull. There are four pair of sinuses lined with a continuous membrane through which they are intercon-

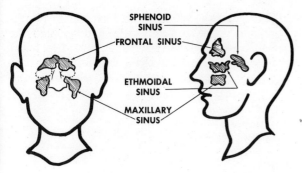

The Sinuses

nected to the nose. If the sinus openings should become blocked by mucous or inflamation, the relative vacuum within the sinus cavities caused by diving will result in pain, discomfort, and nosebleed.

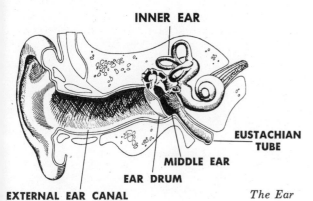

The Ear

THE EAR

When sound-vibrations reach the outer ear, they spill into the external ear canal and set the ear drum vibrating. Its vibrations cause the tiny bones *(hammer, anvil and stirrup)* to vibrate. The stirrup's vibrations are in turn transmitted to the cochlea, where the auditory nerve picks up the signals and carries them to the brain.

The middle ear is the small air space behind the ear drum. It is connected to the pharynx at the rear of the nose through the *eustachian tube,* a small tube about one and a half inches long.

Its function is to maintain a pressure balance between the middle ear and the pressure outside the ear drum.

The inner ear contains the three semi-circular canals which are filled with fluid and lined with tiny hair-like nerve endings. Each canal is in a different plane of motion: 1) rotational 2) front to back, and 3) side to side. The fluid's motion across the tiny hairs is interpreted as movement in any plane and greatly aids our sense of balance.

SMOKING

Cigarette smoking is an obvious health hazard. In addition to its well publicized relationship to lung cancer and chronic bronchitis, cigarette smoking has proven to be a strong factor in fatal bronchopulmonary disease and cardiovascular disease.

If it is possible, smoking is an even greater danger to the diver.

Smoking causes a chronic inflammation of the bronchial lining and jams the lung's airways with an excess of bronchial mucous. Substantial evidence supports the warning that such a restriction of the airways could very well cause air embolism . . . despite the fact that the diver exhaled throughout the ascent and did everything else correctly!

As though that weren't enough, the diver who smokes is less tolerant of the effects of cold water, and far more susceptible to hypoxia, decompression sickness, overexertion, and fatigue to name but a few attendant problems of smoking and diving.

There is no compromise with smoking. If you want to protect your health, quit smoking!

For purposes of classification and simplicity, the medical problems of diving have been divided into:

    a) UNDER PRESSURE *(Problems on Descent)*
    b) ON THE BOTTOM *(Problems at Depth)*
    c) BUBBLE TROUBLE *(Problems on Ascent)*

QUESTIONS ON CHAPTER 4

1. List the natural air containing spaces of the body. Why must they be equalized?
2. Describe the basic structure of the lungs.
3. Explain the function of the alveoli.
4. What is the function of hemoglobin in the blood?
5. What is meant by: a) External Respiration b) Internal Respiration?
6. What is meant by: a) Greater Circulation b) Lesser Circulation?
7. Define "residual volume".
8. Describe the sinuses.
9. What is the eustachian tube and of what importance is it to divers?
10. What is the function of the semi-circular canals?

"If the pressure in their ears got too strong, they were to swallow. If this was not enough, they were to press their noses against the glass to shut off both nostrils, and then blow hard. This second rule I had discovered in a diving textbook, and we concluded that the author must have had a most unusual nose."

Hans Hass, *"Diving to Adventure"*

Chapter 5   UNDER PRESSURE

The Hydro-Lab, the undersea habitat pictured on the opposite page, rests on the ocean floor off Freeport, Grand Bahama Island.

It is being used for a wide range program of medical and scientific studies in a joint venture of Perry Oceanographics, the Bahamas Undersea Research Foundation and the Underwater Explorers Society and for the first time, sport divers will be able to participate in the saturation dives. Though Hydro-Lab is in shallow water, it may well lead to vastly deeper projects on the Continental Shelf; perhaps to 1,000 feet where the total pressure on a diver will be over 575 tons!

As we know, the body is largely fluid, and external pressure is transmitted freely through the body fluids exactly counter-balancing the ambient pressure.

Provided the pressure exerted on the body's natural air spaces is being balanced by air at equal pressure from the diver's breathing unit, and provided this air has free, unobstructed access to all these air spaces, there will be no differential of pressure. Should these air spaces not be equalized however, as little as one p.s.i. of pressure differential can cause congestion, swelling, and bleeding.

Barotrauma is a term which describes any injury resulting from an inability to equalize pressure between a closed air space and the ambient water pressure.

SQUEEZE

Squeeze is probably the most descriptive word in the diver's vocabulary. It describes the affects of unequalized pressure on the body's natural air spaces and the attached air spaces of suit and mask.

Recalling Boyle's Law, which basically states that on descent the volume of a gas will decrease in proportion to increasing absolute pressure, it is obvious that squeeze only occurs when a pressure differential exists between the water and air spaces.

EAR SQUEEZE

When the diver leaves the surface, the middle ear contains air at atmospheric pressure. As the ambient pressure increases with depth, the external pressure will normally be equalized by air passing into the middle ear through the eustachian tube.

If this tube is swollen due to cold, infection, or allergy, the middle ear will not be equalized and a pressure differential will result across the flexible eardrum.

The external pressure will cause the eardrum to deflect inwardly, reducing the volume of air in the middle ear. At the same time, the ambient pressure is being transmitted through the body fluids. Since a relative vacuum is set up in the middle ear, the blood vessels will enlarge and finally leak blood into the middle ear to equalize the pressure differential.

Unfortunately, the eardrum is a relatively delicate tissue and as little as four p.s.i. *(8 feet of water)* of pressure differential can cause it to rupture. If this point of pressure differential is reached, the eardrum will be fully deflected; blood vessels within it will ooze blood. If the descent is continued, the membrane will finally rupture.

Although there are rare people who are insensitive to developing ear squeeze, for most divers the process is extremely painful. Usually, there is sufficient discomfort in just a few feet of descent, to warn the diver before serious damage can occur.

RUPTURE IN COLD WATER

The temperature of the fluid flowing through the semi-circular canals in the internal ear is

98.6°F. If the eardrum ruptures and cold water enters the middle ear, this normal temperature drops rapidly. The balance mechanism is thrown completely haywire and severe dizziness, nausea, and a complete loss of balance may result. This condition is termed *vertigo*.

Because the volume of water that actually enters the middle ear is small, it is quickly warmed to body temperature and normal balance is restored.

Under the circumstances, the best advice to be given is simply, "hang in there." Although the victim literally doesn't know which end is up, if he only waits a minute the violent waves of nausea and dizziness will disappear.

TREATMENT

Any serious ear problem requires competent medical treatment. A sterile cotton plug should be inserted into the ear canal and a doctor's assistance secured. Even serious ruptures will heal within a week or two, barring infection. All diving activity must be discontinued until the doctor gives the green light. Deafness may result from repeated eardrum damage.

PREVENTION

With the exception of those people who can never "equalize" because of a growth or obstruction in the eustachian tube, the usual clearing problems stem from congestion due to colds or allergies.

Few divers are blessed with really open eustachian tubes. Most of us have to help nature by using any one of a number of methods. Among them are swallowing, wiggling the jaw from side to side, or yawning. Perhaps the most positive method is the Valsalva maneuver, pinching the nostrils and exhaling through the nose.

Ear clearing should begin the moment the diver begins his descent and should continue until he is at the selected depth whether there is discomfort or not.

If pain is felt, stop descending. Ascend a few feet to relieve some of the external pressure and "clear" at that level before continuing down.

EAR PLUGS

The use of ear plugs when diving is definitely taboo. Water pressure may drive them deep into the ear canals causing no end of problems.

EXTERNAL EAR INFECTION

Certain people display an unfortunate predisposition to ear infections after repeated diving. The external ear canal being dark, warm and moist is particularly well suited for promoting the multiplication of bacteria. I enthusiastically endorse a product called "Domeboro" which is essentially an acetic acid solution which requires a prescription. After a dive, fill one ear and remain motionless for five minutes. Then, roll over and do the same with the other ear. This simple procedure should keep your ears infection free.

SINUS SQUEEZE

As external pressure builds up during descent, internal pressure is normally transmitted to the sinuses to equalize the ambient pressure.

If the sinus membrane is swollen or the sinus passages obstructed, the sinuses may be shut off from the equalizing internal pressure preventing equalization.

As this pressure differential increases, the "squeezed" sinus produces a sharp pain best described as a "wedging" sensation. Such pain would normally prevent further descent.

Immediate relief results upon ascent. Should the diver ignore this pain and descend even further, the internal pressure will *(as described in ear squeeze)* be transmitted through the body fluids causing the sinus membrane to swell, and finally hemorrhage into the sinus cavity.

Occasionally a diver may return to the surface with a little blood in his mask after being apparently successful in equalizing the sinuses.

A little blood mixed with a lot of water, sloshing around in the bottom of a mask, can give the *impression* of a lot of blood.

A few of the tiny capillaries in the sinus membrane have ruptured and the bleeding should stop soon after surfacing.

If the bleeding should persist, medical attention is required. Diving is not permitted until the sinuses are completely healed.

PREVENTION

As is true of most physiological problems of diving, squeeze need never happen because it is so easy to avoid.

When suffering from a cold, or congested nose, do not dive. Unlike the eustachian tube, the sinus openings are impossible to stretch or distort. This makes pressure equalization difficult when they are obstructed. The sinuses generally have to equalize naturally.

TOOTH SQUEEZE

Although rare, tooth squeeze may result from a small air pocket under a filling or capped tooth. The trapped air is under atmospheric pressure. Upon descent, as pressure mounts around the affected tooth, the tooth walls are compressed. If the air pocket is large enough and external pressure sufficiently high, the tooth could implode.

Even if internal pressure has access to the air pocket, the passage may be too small to allow rapid equalization.

If severe tooth pain is noticed on descent the diver should surface and see his dentist.

Treatment usually involves the replacement of the filling or cap of the affected tooth.

INTESTINAL SQUEEZE

We normally discount the possibility of squeeze on this natural air space. Because of its length and the elasticity of its soft walls, the intestine is simply compressed by the greater ambient pressure. Gas produced by gas-forming foods or inadvertent swallowing of air is easily compressed in the flexible intestine and offers no problem on descent.

Thoracic Squeeze

THORACIC SQUEEZE

When U. S. Navy petty officer, Bob Croft made his record deep dive of 240 feet, he became something of a human phenomenon.

A 240 feet dive isn't generally considered a record deep dive unless you happen to do it Croft's way . . . without breathing apparatus.

Diving physiologists immediately perked up their ears and ran tests on this extraordinary diver. Laboratory tests disclosed that Croft's lung capacity was approximately 16 pints, or about six more than average!

Breath Holding

Although there is a remote possibility that thoracic squeeze may occur if a scuba diver holds his breath or loses his air supply during descent, it is most commonly associated with a deep skin dive *(breath holding)*.

As the skin diver descends, the external water pressure will compress his lungs more and more until the chest walls are completely contracted and the diaphragm is forced fully upwards.

Since there is no source of internal balancing pressure, the lungs are compressed into their normal residual volume. This was earlier defined as the amount of air normally retained in the lungs after the most forceful of exhalations.

Complications

Further descent will produce lung *(thoracic)* squeeze. Already compressed as much as they can naturally, additional external pressure now will force the blood vessels in the lung membrane to hemorrhage into the lung alveoli attempting to equalize pressure by "bleeding."

Under the most extreme circumstances, if descent is continued, forceful and fatal implosion of the thorax could occur.

The critical zone for severe thoracic squeeze for the average skin diver would be in the range of 132 feet of depth.

This arbitrary danger zone is based on the fact that at 132 feet *(5 atmospheres)* the average diver's lung capacity *(10 pints)* will be reduced to one fifth *(2 pints)* . . . less than his normal residual volume.

Incidentally, Bob Croft's previous record dive was cut short at 217 feet 6 inches because he wasn't able to equalize the painful pressure on his ears.

ATTACHED AIR SPACES

Most of this chapter has been taken up by descriptions of the effects of unequalized pressure on the body's natural air spaces. We have yet to deal with the balance of the diver's air spaces, those produced by equipment worn by the diver.

MASK SQUEEZE (FACE)

Normally during a dive, the diver exhales short puffs of air into his mask during descent to keep it from being forced against his face by the external water pressure.

If the diver fails to puff into his mask on descent and the air space between the face and the mask is not equalized with the surrounding water pressure, a severe squeeze may result.

The tiny capillaries in the skin just under the mask hemorrhage giving the face a red "blush." The eyes may become extremely bloodshot and swollen as a result of capillary hemorrhage within the eyes.

Since the only prevention for mask squeeze is exhaling air into the mask to balance the external pressure, it is obvious that since diving goggles *(which cover the eyes only)* cannot be equalized their use will surely lead to eye squeeze.

HOOD SQUEEZE (EXTERNAL EAR)

Although the "dry" type exposure suit has been out of favor for some time, it appears to be making a substantial comeback and its popularity among sport divers is increasing.

When using a dry suit, the hood is usually sealed over the upper flange of the mask. In this way, the diver is enabled to inflate the hood slightly by exhaling into the mask and forcing air directly into the hood. The external water pressure is thereby equalized.

When the diver dresses at the surface, atmospheric *(14.7 p.s.i.)* air is trapped in the external ear canal by the tight fitting hood which seals over the external ear.

On descent, air breathed from the breathing apparatus is transmitted to the middle ear at ambient pressure, while the air pocket in the external ear canal remains at atmospheric pressure.

As in internal ear squeeze, the ear drum is deflected toward the lower pressure and the ambient pressure is transmitted through the body fluids.

As this squeeze worsens, the ear drum deflects and the capillaries in the eardrum and membrane lining the external ear canal leak blood into the air space. If the descent continues, the ear drum will rupture outwardly.

CAROTID ARTERY CONSTRICTION

The fit of any diving suit should be given careful attention. Proper suit fit requires full and comfortable expansion of chest and must in no way impair breathing. Particularly important is the fit of hood and suit collar around the throat and neck. It must be comfortably snug, but not tight.

Gently press your finger tips against the side of your neck just below the ear between the trachea and the neck muscles. Your fingers are over the carotid artery and you *should* be feeling the pulsations of the artery (carotid pulse).

Anytime excessive pressure is applied to this region, the blood flow to the brain will be slowed or even completely interrupted. Indeed, the use of this "pressure point" is a common first aid stop-gap measure in head injury cases to control arterial hemorrhage.

The result of an excessive restriction in this region is faintness, headache, dizziness and the strong possibility of black out.

SUIT SQUEEZE (BODY)

The "dry suit" is an over-sized exposure suit which encases the diver's body in an envelope of air. As the diver descends, the increasing ambient pressure tends to flatten the suit to the body's natural contours.

The dry suit in itself doesn't keep the body warm. It only prevents the surrounding water from conducting away the body heat. It is "oversized" to accommodate insulating layers of thermal underwear which are worn underneath.

As a result, small air pockets are created between the skin and the suit, usually in creases formed by the gathering of excess material where the suit does not fit snugly.

Normally, no problem occurs since the diver can equalize pressure in these air pockets in the manner described in the section on hood squeeze.

The diver's skin tends to be caught in these folds, and if the external pressure is not equalized, the skin is pinched by the compression of the dry suit.

In most cases, this pinching sensation will be sufficiently painful to alert the diver.

Severe suit squeeze, although not considered

particularly hazardous, can result in massive welts and skin hemorrhages.

CAUTION

A diver wearing a dry suit must equalize these air pockets periodically on descent by exhaling into the suit.

It should be remembered that, in accordance with Boyle's Law, the air blown into the suit at depth *(under pressure)* will expand upon ascent and must be vented.

If it isn't, the diver may find the air trapped in the suit overexpanding rapidly, floating him to the surface in an uncontrolled ascent.

If the dry suit overexpands on ascent, the diver can quickly vent the excess air by pulling the sides of the hood away from his face or by extending an arm over his head and pulling the cuff away from his wrist.

Care should be exercised when working in the head down position. If enough air is trapped in the suit, it will rise to the feet, inflate them and possibly carry the upside-down diver helplessly to the surface.

QUESTIONS ON CHAPTER 5

1. Explain the importance of Boyle's Law in diving.
2. Define barotrauma.
3. Describe ear squeeze giving its cause and prevention.
4. Explain the "Valsalva" maneuver.
5. What is vertigo (spatial disorientation)? Give the possible causes.
6. While swollen sinus membranes can be successfully reduced with the use of decongestants, it is generally considered a risky procedure in diving. Why?
7. If a skin diver's lungs contained 10 pints of air at the surface, what would their volume be after a breath-holding dive to a depth of 132 feet in sea water?
8. Describe thoracic squeeze.
9. How does a diver prevent mask squeeze?
10. How can suit squeeze be avoided?

"I can assure you it [oxygen poisoning] is entirely painless to the victim . . . in fact, just before the attack there is a general feeling of well-being. I am told my last words were, 'I don't need help, there is nothing wrong with me.' Then all went black."

Commander Francis D. Fane U.S.N., *"The Naked Warriors"*

Chapter 6   ON THE BOTTOM

In contrast to the previous chapter which dealt with problems arising from the compressive forces of water, this chapter is devoted to problems resulting from the physiological effects of pressure.

These effects are a product of the increased partial pressures of the gases contained in the diver's breathing apparatus *(Dalton's Law)* and the increased absorption of gases by the body fluids at depth. *(Henry's Law)*

Recalling Dalton's and Boyle's Laws, it is obvious that greater air pressures at increasing depths mean more molecules of each component gas in every cubic foot of air. At 33 feet, for example, there are twice as many molecules of oxygen in each cubic foot of air as there are at sea level. And at 132 feet *(an absolute pressure of 5 atmospheres)* there would be five times as many oxygen molecules, the equivalent of breathing pure oxygen at the surface.

The partial pressures of the other component gases will increase in the same proportion. The partial pressure of carbon monoxide and other contaminants will also increase as depth increases, thereby increasing their toxic effects.

Henry's Law states the amount of gas which will go into solution in the blood and body fluids, is in direct proportion to the partial pressure of that gas. At 132 feet, for example, the partial pressure of nitrogen is quintupled. Therefore, five times the amount of nitrogen will be dissolved in the blood at 132 feet as will be held in solution at the surface. A diver, thus "nitrogenated," must eliminate this excess nitrogen as he rises to the surface. A complete discussion of problems on ascent is included in the following chapter, "BUBBLE TROUBLE."

NITROGEN NARCOSIS (RAPTURE OF THE DEPTHS)

As a diver breathing compressed air descends, the partial pressure of nitrogen increases in direct proportion to the depth. At a depth of about 150 feet, there may be noticeable effects as the high partial pressure of nitrogen affects the central nervous system.

Although a state of mild light-headedness may begin in as little as 33 feet, generally the narcotic *(anesthetic)* symptoms are first noticed in the 150 feet range.

The sensations are similar to alcoholic intoxication, beginning with mental confusion and impaired judgment. Any task requiring calculation, judgment or manual skill will reveal this impairment.

MARTINI'S LAW

"Under usual conditions, the effect induced by nitrogen intoxication at 100 feet is comparable to the effect of one dry martini on an empty stomach. At 50 feet increments thereafter, the effect is one additional martini for every 50 feet of descent." This somewhat imperfect law establishes a relationship between nitrogen narcosis and alcoholic intoxication. The obvious point being, the emotionally unstable diver or the individual with a low alcoholic tolerance is likely to be most susceptible to nitrogen drunkenness.

INDIVIDUAL SUSCEPTIBILITY

Just as there is considerable individual variation in tolerance to alcohol, there is also a good deal of difference in susceptibility to nitrogen narcosis.

Nitrogen Narcosis

A few divers may be seriously hampered in as little as 100 feet, while most divers, although somewhat impaired, function reasonably well in the 125 - 175 foot range.

If you have any question about your personal impairment, try converting a light meter reading to a lens setting at 175 feet, or calculating your remaining air supply. You'll find that these ordinarily simple tasks may take five times as long as when done at the surface.

Nitrogen narcosis can be a treacherous problem since some divers may become quite drunk without realizing it. Although time at depth is not an important factor, the greater the depth, the more intense the effect.

Narcosis apparently occurs in three stages. In stage 1, the primary nerve centers are affected. The effect is a mild, pleasant drunkenness. The diver swims in complete bliss. In stage 2, the secondary nerve centers are affected. The diver's inhibitions are released and he may swim off to race a fish, or perhaps even think he is a fish. In stage 3, the lower nerve centers are affected. The diver is completely relaxed and lapses into total submission . . . to the point of losing his sense of self preservation.

There appear to be two distinct types of narcosis. The first, Rapture of the Depths, seems to be a euphoric, joyous sensation of well-being. This is usually associated with warm, clear waters.

On the other hand, divers descending over 200 feet to the wreck of the Andrea Doria in the cold, dark Atlantic have referred to this narcosis as a sensation of depression, melancholy and gloomy fear.

In all cases, narcosis reduces logical thinking. The effects become so pronounced that most divers will be ineffective and a menace to themselves at depths beyond 250 feet.

MECHANISM

The exact reason for the occurrence of Nitrogen Narcosis is unknown. Nitrogen's great solubility in the lipid *(fatty)* tissue may account for part of it, since lipid is an important component of brain tissue.

Diving physiologists come to sword's points over the question of carbon dioxide retention in body tissues as a possible factor in narcosis. There is sufficient evidence to indicate that further experimentation is worthwhile.

PREVENTION

If nitrogen narcosis is suspected or if its development begins, start your ascent immediately. On ascent into shallower water the excessive partial pressure of nitrogen will be reduced and the narcosis dissipated. There are no after-effects or hangover and recovery is complete.

In the interest of safety, the sport diver should limit his dives to a depth of less than 150 feet.

OXYGEN POISONING

Earlier, we described oxygen as the only gas capable of supporting life and essential for the metabolic process. When breathed at high partial pressure however, oxygen can produce dangerous effects.

Even hospital patients are not permitted to breathe pure *(100%)* oxygen. Extended periods *(14 to 24 hours)* of breathing pure oxygen may cause serious lung irritation.

Oxygen poisoning is a convulsive reaction caused by breathing compressed oxygen in a depth-pressure range of about two atmospheres *(33 feet)*.

The sport diver, contrary to the popular misconception, does not charge his tanks with compressed *oxygen*, but compressed air.

There is a breathing apparatus which does utilize pure oxygen, however, and the sport diver should be familiar with it, if only from a standpoint of accident prevention.

REBREATHER

The *closed-circuit rebreather* delivers pure oxygen to the diver and recycles his exhausted breath through a cannister of chemical absorbent which theoretically "scrubs" the carbon dioxide from each exhalation. The purified oxygen is then rebreathed. The diver periodically replenishes the oxygen supply by valving an additional shot of oxygen into the breathing bag. This apparatus is covered in detail in the chapter titled, "THE BUBBLE MACHINE." It can be a dangerous piece of equipment and is definitely *not recommended* for sport diving.

OPEN CIRCUIT

The sport diver using open-circuit scuba needn't worry about oxygen poisoning provided he charges the cylinder with only compressed *air* and, he confines his diving activities to safe depths.

The diver breathing compressed air could possibly reach a depth where the partial pressure of oxygen would be at the critical level of two atmospheres.

For example, a diver breathing compressed air at *297 feet* would be exposed to the same partial pressure of oxygen *(29.4 p.s.i.a.)* as a diver using 100% oxygen at 33 feet *(29.4 p.s.i.a.)*.

MECHANISM

Extensive research notwithstanding, the reason why life-sustaining oxygen will induce convulsions under these circumstances remains a complex problem.

The most serious manifestation of oxygen poisoning is the convulsion, which is similar to the spastic thrashing and jerking of an epileptic seizure. Although these convulsions most frequently occur without warning, other symptoms *may* develop as the high partial pressure begins to affect the nervous and muscular systems.

The time span bridging the first symptom and the onset of convulsions will be quite short, but if the diver immediately reduces the partial pressure of oxygen by ascending to the surface, he may prevent the convulsion.

The symptoms *(again, not necessarily in their order of occurrence)* are nausea, muscle twitching, dizziness, visual and mental disturbances, and respiratory distress.

The occurrence of convulsions apparently depends on two factors, depth and duration of the dive. Experience has shown that individual susceptibility varies tremendously. Prospective Navy divers must demonstrate an average tolerance to pure oxygen for 30 minutes in a recompression chamber at a depth-pressure of 60 feet. The few applicants that don't make it are washed out of the diving program.

TREATMENT

The great danger of a convulsion underwater is, of course, that the diver may injure himself or drown. If a victim is brought promptly to the surface, no treatment is required. The symptoms quickly disappear, followed by apparently complete recovery.

PREVENTION

The sport diver can easily avoid oxygen poisoning. All he need do is insure that his open-circuit scuba tanks are filled with only compressed air. He should never use an oxygen rebreather under any circumstances.

Much has been written regarding the limits for pure oxygen diving. Generally all manuals carry an underscored warning: *"When breathing pure oxygen, never descend below 25 feet."*

Perhaps an equally important rule would be: *"Heavy exertion (and the resultant carbon dioxide excess) should be avoided on pure oxygen dives."* Most authorities generally agree that carbon dioxide sensors may be partially responsible for the onset of oxygen poisoning.

HYPOGLYCEMIA

Under prolonged heavy underwater exercise, hypoglycemia (unusually low blood sugar level) may be brought about by the body's excessive utilization of glucose. Sugar (glucose), the body's principal fuel, is obtained from the food we eat and diving on an empty stomach can substantially reduce the blood sugar level. While blood sugar levels vary considerably from diver to diver, the performance of almost everyone will be affected if prolonged diving is undertaken without the benefit of a good, sustaining meal. The effects of hypoglycemia vary widely. However, the initial symptoms may include hunger, anxiety, alternating chills and profuse perspiration. In severe cases the victim may suffer vertigo, confusion, delerium, convulsions and possibly, loss of consciousness. Diabetics are particularly susceptible to hypoglycemia.

Prevention lies in simply preparing for a dive as you would any demanding sport; eat a good, high protein meal beforehand. At the first sign of fatigue, terminate the dive.

CARBON DIOXIDE EXCESS

It is impossible to overemphasize the need for the recreational diver to breathe properly. It is vitally important that the diver — whether on snorkel or scuba — breathe fully and continuously, taking slow, deep breaths.

Carbon dioxide excess (hypercapnia) will occur anytime the diver's breathing rate is too low to eliminate the carbon dioxide produced by the body. The effects of hypercapnia — depending on the concentration of CO_2 in the body — could be spontaneous and fatal.

It is a serious concern for military divers using closed or semi-closed rebreathers whose carbon dioxide absorbing chemicals may be exhausted or defective.

The elimination of pockets of poor ventilation, so-called "dead spaces" where carbon dioxide could accumulate, is an important design consideration in the development of lightweight helmets and full face mask apparatus.

Although a remote possibility, carbon dioxide could also originate in a poorly maintained air compressor and diving cylinders might be charged with air containing carbon dioxide.

A more probable cause among scuba divers is the idiotic practice of "skip breathing". Some misguided divers restrict their breathing to conserve air — frequently, in an attempt to make their air supply outlast that of their buddy's. Skip breathing (breath holding between shallow breaths) really amounts to self-inflicted hypercapnia by intentionally interferring with the normal elimination of carbon dioxide.

OVEREXERTION

Most sport divers, thankfully, are not suicidal. And yet many, otherwise sensible divers tend to forget that diving should be a slow and energy-saving activity.

The smart diver moves slowly under water. He knows there are a multitude of things to see and do on even the smallest of reefs. Occasionally, you will see some uninformed divers blasting about from reef to reef hurrying to see as much as possible before their air runs out. Of course, they forget that hard swimming burns oxygen ten times as fast as, for example, sitting quietly by a coral head filming reef fish.

And even normal breathing through a regulator is not the same as breathing at the surface. There is some resistance in the finest regulator manufactured. If the diver works or swims hard enough to "run out of breath," particularly if he's not in good physical condition, he'll have to stop and allow his breathing to catch up. And it may take awhile to get all the air his lungs are demanding. For the novice diver, this can be a traumatic experience. The breathless diver is close to panic and may drown.

EFFECTS

A normal increase in carbon dioxide stimulates the respiratory center in the brain which, in turn, triggers an increased breathing rate. An abnormal rise of CO_2 will affect all tissue, particularly that of the brain which is especially susceptible.

Brain function impairment manifests itself in a number of dramatic symptoms. The victim may feel drowsy, dizzy, nauseous or confused. His breathing rate is sure to be altered. Blood pressure and heart rate are significantly increased.

The effects are determined to a large extent by the concentration of CO_2 in the body.

If at atmospheric pressure the carbon dioxide level reaches 2%, the breathing rate will increase, attempting to normalize the concentration. A continued escalation to 5% would cause noticeable panting and general discomfort.

The diver, because of this labored breathing and increasing concentration of carbon dioxide, will quickly become exhausted. If the carbon dioxide level rises to 8%, he will suffer extreme respiratory distress. If the CO_2 level climbs to 10%, the diver will lose consciousness.

The most distinctive sign of carbon dioxide excess is cyanosis — bluish-black coloring of the skin, lips and fingernails.

DEPTH—AN IMPORTANT FACTOR

Depth will increase the partial pressure of carbon dioxide and its detrimental effects. At a depth of 132 feet, for example, the partial pressure of carbon dioxide would be five times its partial pressure at sea level. As little as 2% of carbon dioxide in the breathing air will activate the respiratory center, causing the diver's breathing rate to increase. This itself can be an excellent indicator for carbon dioxide buildup. The CO_2 percentages are approximate for an average adult male.

TREATMENT

Although death as a direct result of carbon dioxide excess is unlikely, the loss of consciousness underwater could lead to drowning. Treatment consists of removing the victim from the water and administering cardiopulmonary resuscitation or simply exposing the victim to fresh air if he is breathing. If an oxygen resuscitator is available, it can quickly purge the excess carbon dioxide and restore the normal oxygen level.

PREVENTION

At atmospheric pressure a carbon dioxide level of only 3% is the maximum tolerated without respiratory problems and must never be exceeded.

If the diver experiences difficulty in breathing, he must stop whatever work he is performing until normal breathing is restored. Exercise will only produce more carbon dioxide and aggravate the condition.

It is worth mentioning that while the symptoms described are generally considered normal, a few divers may not respond to carbon dioxide excess as indicated. The best prevention for carbon dioxide excess is obviously to understand and avoid its causes.

HYPERVENTILATION

Hyperventilation is the practice of "blowing off" the normal carbon dioxide level in the body, by ventilating the lungs through a series of deep inhalations and exhalations.

In the past, spearfishermen practiced hyperventilation prior to a breath-holding dive to extend underwater time.

Although hyperventilation doesn't significantly increase the body's oxygen level, blowing off carbon dioxide and decreasing the respiratory stimulus could dangerously increase the diver's underwater time.

Breathing is stimulated by three basic "triggers." The main trigger is a high carbon dioxide level. To lesser degrees, breathing is also triggered by a low partial pressure of oxygen and decreased lung volume.

On a long breathholding dive, after hyperventilating, the diver's oxygen tension can fall to a dangerously low level before the carbon dioxide "breakpoint" is reached.

A diver, thus unstimulated, could hold his breath until he is on the verge of becoming hypoxic before the urge to breathe becomes noticeable.

SHALLOW WATER BLACKOUT

Shallow water blackout is a term originally coined by Royal British Navy divers to describe a sudden loss of consciousness resulting from defective CO_2 absorbents in closed-circuit, oxygen rebreathers.

Currently, however, the term shallow water blackout has become analagous with a phenomenon of spontaneous unconsciousness resulting from latent hypoxia or hyperventilation syndrome.

MECHANISM

The diver's breathholding time is extended considerably by the depth of the dive. The partial pressure of oxygen increases in direct proportion to the depth. The body uses oxygen in terms of actual molecules rather than volume. As a result, the body's consumption of oxygen does not increase with depth.

A diver filling his lungs at the surface will have a partial pressure of oxygen of about 2/10 of an atmosphere.

Diving to 99 feet, the partial pressure of oxygen would be four times as great *(8/10 of one atmosphere)*. The skin diver may have an adequate partial pressure of oxygen to remain at 99 feet for as long as three minutes.

While he is holding his breath, the diver's body tissues continue to burn the oxygen in proportion to his exertion. The harder he swims, the faster the oxygen is used and more carbon dioxide is generated. Through training, the diver may become insensitive to the usual CO_2 "triggers," thereby enabling the oxygen level to drop dangerously low.

By the time the diver feels the need to breathe and starts his ascent, the decreasing water pressure will allow the partial pressure of oxygen to drop rapidly to hypoxic levels. The corresponding drop in CO_2 partial pressure at the same time may give the diver a false sense of relief from the urge to breathe. The diver will become a victim of hypoxia before he can reach the surface.

HYPOXIA

Hypoxia has been defined as a lack of oxygen available to the body tissues. This lack of oxygen will interrupt the normal function of all body cells and, if not corrected, will cause their eventual death. The brain tissue is highly sensitive to oxygen deprivation. If the brain cells are without oxygen for as little as thirty seconds, they may be seriously affected. Permanent damage may result from as little as two minutes of oxygen starvation.

Although hypoxia can be brought about through improper use of the closed-circuit oxygen rebreather *(which is fully discussed in a later chapter)* under normal circumstances it is improbable in open-circuit scuba diving.

It is the breathholding skin diver who is most apt to experience hypoxia. And usually as a result of excessive hyperventilation.

HYPERVENTILATION SYNDROME

Hyperventilation Syndrome describes a condition of unintentional abnormally rapid, shallow breathing. This condition may be precipitated by the so-called "distraction effect" of sudden immersion in extremely cold water or any condition (e.g. overexertion) which increases the body's demand for oxygen. Perhaps the most common cause of hyperventilation syndrome is stress-triggered anxiety.

It is important to note that this condition is as likely to affect the snorkel diver on the surface as it is the scuba diver at depth. Indeed, cases have been reported of scuba divers successfully managing an underwater accident and an emergency swimming ascent only to lose consciousness while snorkeling back to the dive boat. Because of the inefficiency of this type of breathing, the body's carbon dioxide tension may be abnormally reduced (hypocapnia) producing symptoms of faintness, dizziness, numbness, tremors or muscle spasms, and if the carbon dioxide debit is extreme, probable loss of consciousness.

Prevention lies mainly in proper breathing, self-control and safe, sensible diving. In the event of involuntary hyperventilation the diver must stop all activity, immediately relax and force the depth rather than the rate of his breathing. In just a short time, the regular breathing rhythm will be reestablished.

SYMPTOMS

In the gradual development of hypoxia, a number of symptoms may appear: mental confusion, inability to concentrate, faulty judgment, impaired muscular control, and emotional instability, followed closely by a sense of euphoria, a medical term for a feeling of unfounded, extreme well-being.

The diver may be cyanotic, as described in CO_2 excess. At this point, he is unable to comprehend his predicament and rapidly loses consciousness. Unless he is rescued from the water, drowning is imminent.

TREATMENT

Like carbon dioxide excess, the treatment should consist of removing the victim from the water and administering mouth-to-mouth resuscitation if required, or simply exposing the victim to fresh air if he is breathing. If an oxygen resuscitator is available, it will quickly restore the normal gas tensions.

PREVENTION

The diver's best prevention for hypoxia is to avoid the use of hyperventilation and to ascend to the surface immediately upon feeling the slightest urge to breathe. When using scuba, breathe normally at all times.

AIR CONTAMINANTS

The scuba diver is, to a large degree, dependent upon the purity of the compressed air which he breathes. He is vulnerable to any toxic substances which may be compressed into his air cylinder through a defective air compressor or filter arrangement. Two of these toxic inhalants are of special importance: carbon monoxide and oil vapor.

CARBON MONOXIDE (CO) POISONING

This highly poisonous gas is a treacherous menace to the unsuspecting diver whose air supply may have been contaminated with this colorless, odorless, and tasteless gas.

This contaminant may enter through the air intake of the air compressor and be compressed with the pure air into the diver's air cylinder. This is a definite possibility where the air intake is located too close to the exhaust of the gasoline engine drive.

Another possibility is the overheating and "dieselizing" of the oil in an oil lubricated compressor. "Dieselizing" in effect means that the compressor has overheated and caused the incomplete combustion of the oil.

MECHANISM

The blood hemoglobin will soak up carbon monoxide at a rate 300 times faster than it will take up oxygen. The red blood cells, loaded with carbon monoxide, are unable to take up any oxygen. The body tissues thus deprived of oxygen, begin to die of oxygen starvation.

At atmospheric pressure, as little as 1,000 PPM *(parts per million)* or 0.1% of carbon monoxide is considered to be a lethal concentration. Increased partial pressures at depth also increase the toxic effects of carbon monoxide. Although no national air standards have yet been established, the *maximum* allowable concentration of carbon monoxide in diving air has been arbitrarily fixed at 10 PPM or 0.001 per cent for non-decompression diving.

WARNING SIGNS

Certain symptoms occur with sufficient regularity in carbon monoxide poisonings to warrant consideration. As carbon monoxide combines with the blood's hemoglobin in the earliest stages, the victim may feel some shortness of breath. As more of this gas is taken up in the blood, the victim may experience slight headache, mild skin flush and tightness across the forehead. At greater concentrations of carbon monoxide severe headache with throbbing at the temples can occur followed by a feeling of weakness, dizziness and nausea. Beyond this, he will begin to breathe rapidly and lapse into coma and convulsions. It is important to note that while these symptoms can and do occur, they are not reliable warnings. Unconsciousness is often the first symptom of carbon monoxide poisoning.

The victim of CO poisoning has one characteristic sign; his skin, lips and fingernails take on a cherry red color.

TREATMENT

The victim must be brought to the surface and mouth-to-mouth resuscitation begun immediately. Exposure to fresh air will generally suffice if the victim is breathing, although administering pure oxygen will flush the carbon monoxide from the body much faster. For example, one half of the carbon monoxide will be purged in 240 minutes breathing air, as compared to 40 minutes if pure oxygen is breathed.

In extreme cases, all attempts must be made to get the victim to a recompression chamber. If the victim is exposed to two atmospheres of pure oxygen, carbon monoxide washout is rapid and chances of complete recovery increased tremendously.

OIL VAPOR

An overheated, oil-lubricated air compressor may charge the compressed air with oil particles. Should the diver breathe this air, the oil vapor may coat the lung alveoli and cause lipoid pneumonia.

The alveoli, thus oil coated, restrict the oxygen exchange in the lungs and the body tissues suffer oxygen starvation.

Normally, the body rejects such foreign matter and it is coughed up and spit out.

Although symptoms are relatively few, the presence of oil accumulation in the lungs can be quickly detected by chest x-ray.

The diver's best warning signal is his delicate sense of smell. Even the slightest trace of oil vapor will cause a distinctive and unpleasant odor easily detected by the sense of smell.

PREVENTION

Though carbon monoxide itself is virtually undetectable by the senses, the impurities that usually accompany CO will cause the air to taste "bad".

If your air has a foul taste or odor, it is a good indication of contaminants and should not be used.

The best advice is to know your air station operator. Does he maintain his compressor carefully? Are his filters changed regularly? For out-of-town trips, a pocket-sized CO indicator is valuable in detecting possible toxic concentrations of carbon monoxide in your air supply. A number of such detectors are available through:

Mine Safety Appliance Company
400 Penn Center Blvd.
Pittsburgh, Pa. 15235

By confining the air sample to a small area (like a sampling bottle), CO concentrations as low as 600 parts per million can be detected with a very inexpensive carbon monoxide detector ampule distributed by M-S-A.

VERTIGO

Spatial disorientation *(Vertigo)* is a disorder in which the diver or his environment seems to whirl dizzily. As described earlier, it may accompany a ruptured eardrum. Yet another cause, which may induce Vertigo in *any* diver, is the loss of a visual point of reference. The diver is particularly susceptible anytime the water is clouded with suspended silt or plankton, or he is at a depth where neither the surface nor bottom is distinguishable.

Under these circumstances the mind may become terribly confused and the diver totally disoriented as to the direction in which he is moving. In severe cases, the diver may become violently nauseated. Occasionally, a diver may experience vertigo when exploring a sunken ship which may lie on the bottom at an unusual angle. A visual illusion is thus created and the diver may orient himself with the tilted deck and discover his exhaust bubbles are trailing away sideways instead of going up.

Since the diver is virtually weightless underwater, the normal balance mechanisms are relatively unreliable. He is largely dependent upon sight to confirm his position in the water and if his eyes betray him, he may find himself confused and disoriented. At this point, he must trust the direction of his bubbles and orient himself accordingly. Fixing the eyes on some stationary object will eliminate the bewildering sensation of vertigo almost immediately.

The experienced diver through training and the resultant confidence is rarely troubled by vertigo.

ASCENT VERTIGO

A peculiar form of vertigo may occur on ascent, particularly after a deep scuba dive, when the diver's middle ear spaces may not depressurize at a rate consistent with the ascent.

The inner ear balance mechanism senses this pressure imbalance and reacts spontaneously giving the diver a sudden wave of vertigo. This phenomenon, though startling, is of no serious consequence if the diver simply slows his ascent giving the sluggish middle ear spaces enough time to depressurize normally.

Equalization can be aided by pinching off the nostrils, inhaling the air through the eustachian tubes and swallowing.

DRUGS, DRINKING AND DIVING

It should be immediately obvious to anyone that the use of alcohol (liquor) and/or any of the current wave of "turn on" drugs (narcotics, hallucinogens, intoxicants, barbituates, etc.) before diving is tantamount to suicide!

Those who might argue against the evidence of impaired judgement, unpredictable behavior, respiratory depression, and blood pressure changes, etc. will take little comfort in a recent study conducted by the University of Michigan. Of 55 random drug purchases made on and off campus, over half contained a dangerous coma-inducing drug which none of the buyers knew he was getting. But the dangers are, or at least should be, clear and obvious.

Not so obvious, however, are the dangers associated with the so-called "non-prescription" drugs that are swallowed routinely and unquestioningly by otherwise sensible citizens.

Some that come immediately to mind are the cough medicines, aspirins, decongestants, and motion sickness preparations. Many cough medicines, for example, commonly include codeine, which while reducing pain also acts as a respiratory depressant.

Aspirins belong to a family of drugs termed *antipyretics* which are used basically to reduce fever by bringing more blood to the skin where it is cooled — and greater amounts of perspiration released. Underwater this transposes to a much more rapid body heat loss.

Decongestants are of unquestionable value in reducing swollen sinus membranes and helping to eliminate the "stopped-up" feeling. These drugs, however, contain antihistamines which can induce sudden drowsiness thereby seriously impairing the diver's ability to think clearly. Should decongestants be used prior to a dive, there is a strong possibility the effect of the drug may wear off while the diver is still at depth. As a result, the sinus membrane will become swollen and trap high pressure air in the sinus cavities. This complication is termed "rebound effect". Upon ascent, the air will expand and may cause internal rupture of the sinus membrane.

Motion sickness preparations also contain antihistamines. Antihistamines act as depressants on the central nervous system. Like the narcotic effect of nitrogen on deep air dives, such depressants affect the primary nerve centers first, producing thick-wittedness and torpor. There is every reason to believe that effects of depressant drugs and nitrogen narcosis are cumulative. That is to say, the diver who has ingested antihistamines is potentially closer to a stage wherein their combined depressant action may paralyze his reflexes of survival.

In summary, there is a clear message in the foregoing. The need for medication may well indicate a dangerous predisposition to illness or injury. Diving places healthy demands on healthy bodies. No dive can justify the potential for injury that exists when attempting to dive when not physically up to par.

QUESTIONS ON CHAPTER 6

1. What is the cause of Nitrogen Narcosis?
2. Describe its effects.
3. Explain the wide range of variation in individual susceptibility.
4. What is the partial pressure of oxygen in air at a depth of 297 feet in sea water?
5. List the possible causes of oxygen poisoning.
6. What are the symptoms of carbon dioxide excess?
7. What is hyperventilation? What are the dangers of hyperventilating? Why is a diver able to hold his breath longer after hyperventilation?
8. What is hypoxia?
9. How does Carbon Monoxide poisoning occur in diving? How is the blood hemoglobin involved?
10. What preventative steps can be taken to avoid vertigo?

"The greater the depth, the longer the stay at the bottom, the more will the blood be charged with an excess of gas in solution. The diver is really, from a physical point of view, like a bottle charged with carbonic acid."

Professor Leroy de Mericourt,
Ann. d'Hygiene Publique et de Medicine Legale, 1860.

Chapter 7   BUBBLE TROUBLE

During ascent, the physiological problems which may occur are the result of decreasing ambient pressure. These problems have been grouped under two categories.

Category I describes the disorders caused by nitrogen being released from solution as bubbles.

Category II describes the disorders caused by air expanding within the body's natural air spaces.

CATEGORY I

DECOMPRESSION SICKNESS — "BENDS"

At the surface, the body fluids have absorbed an amount of nitrogen equal to the partial pressure of nitrogen in air at atmospheric pressure.

As the diver descends, he breathes air at a pressure equal to the surrounding water. Recalling Henry's Law, as the ambient pressure increases more and more nitrogen will be forced into solution in the blood and body fluids.

These gases diffuse through the alveoli into the blood, and are carried to the body tissues.

SATURATION

The amount of gas dissolved in the blood depends upon the *depth* and the *duration* of the dive. When the amount of gas held in solution equals the partial pressure of that gas *(and this may take up to 12 hours)* the body is said to be *saturated* with that gas at that particular depth.

If the diver is at a particular depth for a short duration, a proportionally small amount of gas will be absorbed by the body fluids.

However, once the body is saturated at a particular pressure, the only way more gas can be absorbed is by increasing the ambient pressure *(going still deeper)*. While the diver remains at depth, these gases are held in solution.

NORMAL NITROGEN ELIMINATION (DECOMPRESSION)

Since oxygen is constantly being burned by the body tissues, it presents no problems on ascent. And despite the fact that oxygen, carbon dioxide, and water vapor will also be absorbed by the body fluids, it is principally nitrogen since it constitutes almost 80% of the absorbed gases which must be eliminated from the body on ascent.

As the diver slowly ascends, with a corresponding drop in ambient pressure, the excess gases *(principally nitrogen)* are returned to the lungs in solution, exchanged and eliminated in the normal respiratory cycle. This process is called decompression time or normal nitrogen elimination.

Normal nitrogen elimination takes time, however. To a large degree, the elimination time depends on the depth of the dive, the time at depth and, to a lesser degree, the circulatory efficiency of the diver.

If the body has become so saturated that there is not sufficient time for normal nitrogen elimination during normal ascent and ambient pressure is reduced too quickly, a serious difference between the tension of nitrogen in solution and the ambient pressure occurs.

SUPERSATURATION

If ascent is too rapid and decompression time inadequate to rid the body tissue of excess nitrogen through normal lung ventilation, bubbles of nitrogen will develop in the blood stream and tissues. This condition is termed *supersaturation.*

47

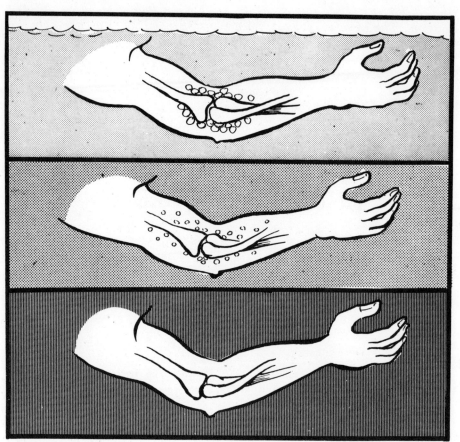

THE BENDS

SUPER SATURATION

SATURATION

Development of the Bends

It is generally agreed that a condition of slight supersaturation can be tolerated and microscopic bubbles may actually form in the tissue with the slightest difference between tissue pressure and surrounding water pressure. This situation is tolerable and the diver will experience no ill effects. The maximum times a diver can spend at the indicated depths without the need for decompression are indicated in the NO DECOMPRESSION LIMITS CHART.

However, anytime the pressure of the dissolved nitrogen in the body rises to more than twice the surrounding water pressure, bubbles developing in the blood stream and tissues will cause decompression sickness. The classic comparison is an uncapped bottle of coke. While capped, carbon dioxide is held in solution in the liquid. Pop the cap and the liquid becomes supersaturated and carbon dioxide now bubbles out of solution. In the human body, the effect is precisely the same as nitrogen boils out of solution in the blood. The greater the difference between the tissue pressure and surrounding water pressure, the larger and more numerous the bubbles of escaping nitrogen.

CO_2 Bubbling Out of Solution

SYMPTOMS

Once nitrogen bubbles develop, their size and their location will determine their effect on the diver. Pain is clearly the most frequent symptom of decompression sickness. Although this pain may begin gradually, it can intensify rapidly to the unbearable stage. The pain is generally localized in the joints, muscles, tendons or ligaments. These bubbles usually occur first in areas of poor circulation, but may appear anywhere in the body. The injury results from the obstruction of the blood's circulation by a bubble. A certain amount of tissue deformation or swelling may occur. If pain is present, it is not likely to be mild. All symptoms will occur within 24 hours of the dive. As a rule, 85 percent of these will occur within one hour and the remaining 15 percent within 12 hours. The term "bends" resulted from deformities caused by the stricken diver's inability to straighten the joints. The diver was literally "bent" out of shape.

THE "STAGGERS"

If bubbles lodge in central nervous system *(brain and spinal cord)* serious consequences will be evidenced by symptoms of visual and auditory disturbances, paralysis, dizziness, convulsions and unconsciousness. These symptoms indicate that some area of the brain or spinal cord is suffering oxygen starvation because of a plug of nitrogen.

THE "CHOKES"

Occasionally, the respiratory system is affected when bubbles lodge in the lungs, causing shortness of breath, severe cough, rapid shallow breathing, unconsciousness and shock. An excellent sign of the "chokes" is an uncontrollable, hacking cough that occurs when the victim takes a deep breath.

THE "ITCHES" (SKIN BENDS)

Intermittent sensations of prickling and burning are common after a deep dive. This itching may accompany a large rash or even large patches of irregular mottling of the skin. The affected area may remain tender to the touch for a few days, then gradually disappear. Bubbles anywhere in the body may cause unusual fatigue after a dive. Although these symptoms usually clear up without treatment, they may precede a serious case of the bends.

The range of symptoms of decompression sickness is so varied that any unexplained symptoms occurring after a dive should be suspected as the bends. If untreated, the slightest case of the bends may result in permanent injury. For the diver who has been "bent", immediate recompression to redissolve the nitrogen bubbles is the only satisfactory treatment.

TREATMENT (RECOMPRESSION AND SURFACE DECOMPRESSION)

If a diver exhibits symptoms of the bends, it is imperative that he be treated in a *recompression chamber*, where the diver is recompressed until the nitrogen bubbles are taken up in the solution in the body tissues and blood. The bubbles are then compressed to non-symptomatic size thus relieving the bends.

The diver is then given surface decompression according to the NAVY STANDARD TREATMENT TABLES.

The pressure is gradually decreased as the dissolved nitrogen is eliminated normally through the lungs, until the diver is returned to surface pressure. The Standard Treatment Tables are so arranged that during surface decompression *(in a recompression chamber)*, the critical ratio of 2 to 1 between the tissue nitrogen tension and the surrounding pressure respectively is never exceeded or even approached.

Stage decompression is quite workable for helmet divers who have an unlimited air supply pumped down from the surface and are brought up in stages by surface control. It is totally impractical for the free-swimming scuba diver with his limited air supply.

It should also be remembered that improper or inadequate treatment will only aggravate the situation, leaving the diver in even worse condition.

Knowing the location of the recompression chamber nearest the diving area and the fastest way of getting to it should be a cardinal rule before any dive.

PREVENTION

When surfacing, the diver must eliminate the excess nitrogen to prevent the body fluids from becoming supersaturated and the resultant nitrogen bubbles. It is eminently simple. The *Navy Standard Decompression Tables* specify "stops" and rate of ascent where the diver has adequate time to get rid of the excess nitrogen.

NAVY STANDARD DECOMPRESSION TABLE (REFER TO THE APPENDIX)

These tables indicate stops on ascent and time intervals at these specified stops required to eliminate nitrogen excess and prevent decompression sickness. A safety factor on dives involving extremely cold water or unusually hard work may be added by going to the depth or time greater than that which would ordinarily be used.

Decompression is a restrictive factor in sport diving. Consider a bounce dive to 150 feet. If the diver returns to the surface within five minuates, no decompression is required. Unfortunately, you can't do much in a 5 minute bounce dive. If our bottom time is extended to 30 minutes, we are faced with 34 minutes of decompression time. Extending our bottom time to 80 minutes would require almost *3 hours* of decompression time!

FAIL-SAFE?

In some diving circles, there is a general misconception that the diving tables are fail-safe and as such can be violated without fear.

The truth is such a decompression table *(one which would be unfailingly safe)* would require even greater time-depth restrictions and longer decompression stops. Such a table would be perfectly safe, but neither necessary nor practical.

The U. S. Navy considers an incidence of decompression sickness of up to 5% acceptable. And this does occur even though the tables are followed to the letter. Of course, there is a recompression chamber on standby at every navy diving operation.

RATE OF ASCENT

The decompression tables are based on a fixed ascent rate of 60 feet per minute. Ascending faster or slower *(in some circumstances)* may lead to the bends.

"NO DECOMPRESSION" LIMITS

The sport diver can avoid decompression sickness easily. Dives requiring decompression stops make diving quite complicated and take much of the fun out of the sport. Planning and preparations are painstaking and require serious attention to detail. Couple all this with the constant risk of running out of air during decompression and it is clear the sport diver should dive within

the "*no decompression*" limits of the standard decompression tables.

The following chart gives dive times at various depths not requiring decompression stops on ascent.

DIVE DEPTH (FEET)	BOTTOM* TIME (MINUTES)
33 (or less)	NO TIME LIMIT
35	310
40	200
50	100
60	60
70	50
80	40
90	30
100	25
110	20
120	15
130	10
140	10
150	5

Bottom Time includes the interval from the moment a diver leaves the surface to the moment he *starts* his ascent, and not just actual time at depth.

No Decompression Limits Chart

REPETITIVE DIVING

While a *single* dive is the first dive of the day, any dive made within 10 minutes to 12 hours of a previous dive is termed a repetitive dive. Every dive leaves some excess nitrogen in the body. This excess is termed residual nitrogen and when more than one dive is made within any 12 hour period, the residual nitrogen effect of those dives is cumulative.

In order that the diver eliminate this excess completely, a period of 12 hours must be spent at the surface to restore the surface equilibrium of the partial pressure of nitrogen.

Since every dive will leave some residual nitrogen in the body, repetitive diving will significantly increase the total amount of nitrogen dissolved in the body. If the diver is not familiar with this phenomenon, he may surface with the "bends". To minimize the need for decompression, schedule all repetitive dives so that each successive dive is performed at a shallower depth.

Included in this book are the U. S. Navy's REPETITIVE DIVE TABLES and WORKSHEETS, a sensible system of determining safe decompression schedules for repetitive dives. Refer to the Appendix.

The basis of this system is the "surface interval", the elapsed time between surfacing from one dive and leaving the surface on a repetitive dive. The surface interval gives credit for the nitrogen eliminated at the surface between dives. The longer the surface interval, the greater the amount of nitrogen eliminated. Repetitive dives made after surface intervals of less than 10 minutes must be considered as a continuation of the previous dive. (Refer to Repetitive Dive Procedures in Appendix B.)

HIGH ALTITUDE DECOMPRESSION

As we have learned, decompression sickness will occur *only* if the pressure of the nitrogen dissolved in the body is raised to *more than* twice the pressure of the surrounding water. To avoid the formation of symptomatic bubbles, we simply ascend at a rate of 60 feet per minute from a no-decompression dive — or — if we have made a dive requiring decompression, we need only make the indicated decompression steps as determined from the U. S. Navy Standard Air Decompression Table. This table is calculated to produce the shortest decompression time possible consistent with safety. When used at sea level, the critical 2 to 1 ratio between tissue nitrogen tension and surrounding water pressure is never exceeded.

Unfortunately, all diving activity does not begin at sea level. Considerable diving activity occurs in high altitude waters like Lake Tahoe (altitude 6,000 feet.)

The standard air tables are predicated on the diver returning to an absolute sea level pressure of 14.7 p.s.i. A diver ascending from a dive in a high altitude lake would return to a pressure less than 14.7 p.s.i. (Refer to the Ambient Pressure Chart) Consequently, the standard air tables alone *cannot* be used safely for diving at high altitudes!

The following conversion tables, when used in conjunction with the standard tables provide the high altitude diver with a safe and practical solution.

Table A assigns theoretical depths for each actual diving depth at various altitudes.

Table B similarly gives the theoretical depth of decompression stops at altitude.

TABLE A
THEORETICAL DEPTH AT ALTITUDE FOR GIVEN ACTUAL DIVING DEPTH IN FRESH WATER

Theoretical Depth at Various Altitudes (in feet)

Actual Depth	1000	2000	3000	4000	5000	6000	7000	8000	9000	10000
0	0	0	0	0	0	0	0	0	0	0
10	10	11	11	12	12	12	13	13	14	15
20	21	21	22	23	24	25	26	27	28	29
30	31	32	33	35	36	37	39	40	42	44
40	41	43	45	46	48	50	52	54	56	58
50	52	54	56	58	60	62	65	67	70	73
60	62	64	67	69	72	75	78	81	84	87
70	72	75	78	81	84	87	91	94	98	102
80	83	86	89	92	96	100	103	108	112	116
90	93	97	100	104	108	112	116	121	126	131
100	103	107	111	116	120	124	129	134	145	145
110	114	118	122	127	132	137	142	148	153	160
120	124	129	134	139	144	149	155	161	167	174
130	135	140	145	150	156	162	168	175	181	189
140	145	150	156	162	168	174	181	188	195	203
150	155	161	167	173	180	187	194	202	209	218
160	166	172	178	185	192	199	207	215	223	232
170	176	182	189	196	204	212	220	228	237	247
180	186	193	200	208	216	224	233	242	251	261
190	197	204	212	220	228	237	246	255	265	276
200	207	215	223	231	240	249	259	269	279	290
210	217	225	234	243	252	261	272	282	293	305
220	228	236	245	254	264	274	284	296	307	319
230	238	247	256	266	276	286	297	309	321	334
240	248	258	267	277	288	299	310	323	335	348
250	259	268	278	289	300	311	323	336	349	363

Reprinted with the permission of Skin Diver magazine and E. R. Cross

Instructions For Use

To find the theoretical diving depth: enter the table horizontally on the exact or next greater actual dive depth. Altitudes to 10,000 feet head the vertical columns. (If the actual altitude falls between tabulated altitudes, use the next higher.) Actual depth and altitude columns intersect at the theoretical depth.

TABLE B
THEORETICAL DEPTH OF DECOMPRESSION STOP AT ALTITUDE

Prescribed Depth	1000	2000	3000	4000	5000	6000	7000	8000	9000	10000
0	0	0	0	0	0	0	0	0	0	0
10	10	9	9	9	8	8	8	7	7	7
20	19	19	18	17	17	16	15	15	14	14
30	29	28	27	26	25	24	23	22	22	21
40	39	37	36	35	33	32	31	30	29	28

Instructions For Use

To convert prescribed depths of decompression stops (designated by U. S. Navy Standard Air Decompression Table) to theoretical depths: enter the table on the exact prescribed depth horizontally. Where exact or next greater altitude and prescribed depth intersect is the theoretical depth of decompression stop.

At sea level, a single dive to a depth of 60 feet for a bottom time of 60 minutes would be a no-decompression dive, thereby permitting returning directly to the surface at 60 feet per minute with no decompression stops.

The same dive in Lake Tahoe, as indicated by the following dive profile, would require 17 minutes of decompression!

Although actual dive depth is 60 feet, the theoretical depth determined from Table A is 75 feet. The U. S. Navy Standard Air Decompression Table specifies using the next greatest depth of 80 feet. A 60 minute bottom time at 80 feet requires 17 minutes of decompression at 10 feet.

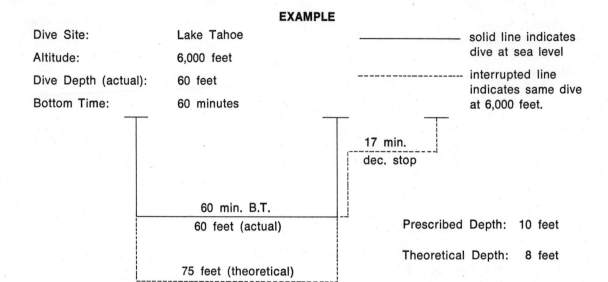

Dive Site: Lake Tahoe

Altitude: 6,000 feet

Dive Depth (actual): 60 feet

Bottom Time: 60 minutes

———————— solid line indicates dive at sea level

- - - - - - - - - interrupted line indicates same dive at 6,000 feet.

17 min.
dec. stop

60 min. B.T.

60 feet (actual)

Prescribed Depth: 10 feet

Theoretical Depth: 8 feet

75 feet (theoretical)

However, the prescribed depth of the decompression stops must also be converted to theoretical depths. The theoretical (corrected) depth of the decompression stop is 8 feet.

NOTE: It is important to remember that for safe decompression, the diver's chest must be held as close as possible to each decompression stop for the required times. Depth gauges must *NEVER* be used to determine decompression stop depths! Many depth gauges, while quite reliable at depth, become dangerously inaccurate in the relatively shallow range of decompression stops. This is particularly true of bourdon tube gauges at high altitudes.

Decompression dives require a heavily weighted descending line clearly labeled with decompression depth markers.

SATURATION DIVING

At present time, divers working for the offshore oil industries are living in undersea dwellings and making dives regularly to 1500 feet and beyond. The divers remain in these undersea stations for periods of several weeks. The system which enables divers to work and live at these great depths is called saturation diving.

These divers spend sufficient time *(24 to 36 hours)* under depth-pressure to become completely saturated with the inert breathing gas *(probably helium)*. Once saturated at a given depth, there is no increase in decompression time regardless of how long the diver remains at that depth. A diver who has been saturated at any depth will require no greater decompression time if he stays down a week or a month.

Saturation diving is conducted for weeks with the men living and working in high-pressure undersea habitats. This technique permits the maximum ratio of working time to decompression time.

Decompression time for such a saturation dive is in the 80 to 90 hour range.

CATEGORY II

During ascent, air in the body's natural air spaces will expand. Normally, this expanding air is vented freely and no difficulties arise. Recalling Boyle's Law, a diver's lungs inflated with compressed air at 33 feet should theoretically expand to twice their original volume if the diver held his breath and ascended to the surface. Unfortunately, the lungs are not at all flexible. If the scuba diver holds his breath on ascent, serious overinflation of the lungs will occur.

AIR EMBOLISM

Provided the diver breathes normally on ascent, the expanding lung air is exhaled unnoticed. If a diver breathing from any source of compressed air underwater holds his breath on ascent, the air trapped in his lungs will expand in proportion to the decreasing ambient pressure. If this expanding air is not exhaled promptly, a pressure differential between the lung air and the water pressure occurs.

When the lungs are fully expanded, a pressure differential of as little as two p.s.i. *(the equiva-*

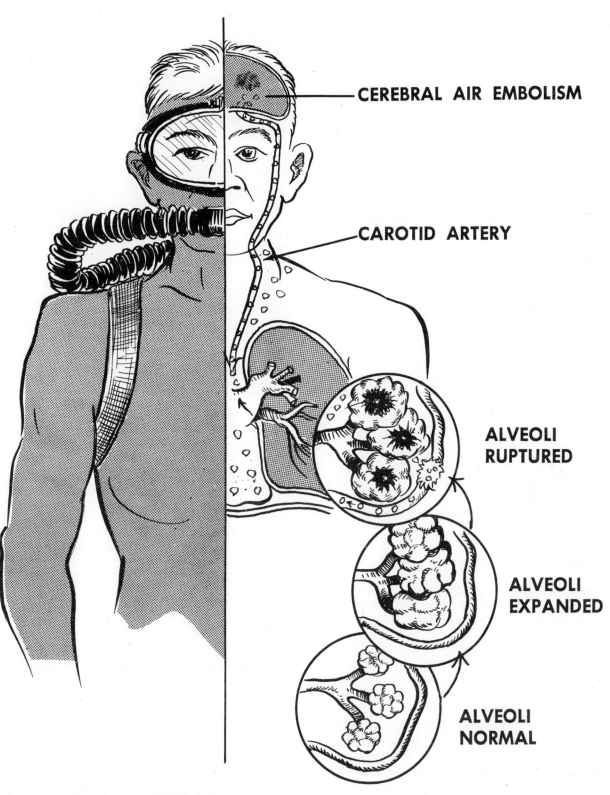

CEREBRAL AIR EMBOLISM

CAROTID ARTERY

ALVEOLI
RUPTURED

ALVEOLI
EXPANDED

ALVEOLI
NORMAL

Development of Air Embolism

lent of about 4 feet of ascent) will overexpand the delicate alveoli and cause them to burst.

MECHANISM

A stream of pressurized air bubbles is forced through the tear into the blood capillaries covering the alveoli. Once in the circulatory system, these bubbles are carried through the heart and into the carotid artery, which carries oxygen-rich blood to the brain.

Eventually, the expanding air bubbles lodge in the brain capillaries, forming a blockage *(embolus)*. This plug of air prevents the blood from reaching the brain tissue. The affected area of the brain, thus deprived of its vital supply of oxygen, can survive only a few minutes without sustaining permanent injury or death of its tissue.

SYMPTOMS

The symptoms of air embolism are sudden and dramatic. The victim may stagger from the water, cough up a bloody froth, appear confused, and collapse. He may be unconscious before reaching the surface. On the other hand, he may appear quite normal for a time, then suddenly lose consciousness. Paralysis and convulsions will generally accompany massive air embolism. Respiratory difficulty, cyanosis, breathing stoppage, or a "pulling" sensation in the mediastinum may also result from the lung damage.

The time elapsed between the onset of the first symptom to possible convulsions may be a matter of minutes.

Any scuba diver brought to the surface unconscious, or who loses consciousness shortly after surfacing, must be regarded as a victim of possible embolism.

TREATMENT

Since the problem involves the brain, where the cells quickly die if deprived of oxygen, it is imperative the victim be rushed to a recompression chamber.

Immediate recompression will force the air bubbles back into solution and if massive brain tissue deterioration has not occurred, the victim stands a good chance of recovering.

Recompression by resubmerging the victim is totally impractical. Treatment may require a depth-pressure equivalent of 165 feet for as long as 38 hours.

While transporting the victim to the nearest recompression chamber, administer mouth to mouth resuscitation if breathing has stopped. Resuscitating with pure oxygen is of definite value.

If heartbeat is not detectable, begin external heart massage at once. The victim should be positioned on his left side with his head lower than his feet at all times to assist restoration of circulation and dispersion of emboli. Keep the victim warm. Wrap him in blankets, if necessary. Treatment must begin *immediately* if the victim is to have a fighting chance to survive.

PREVENTION

The real tragedy of an air embolism is that any diver should suffer this malady, when it is so easy to avoid. Prevention simply requires breathing normally or exhaling throughout ascent. If you are out of air, remember to exhale continuously on ascent.

As one Navy wit suggested:
You can never blow out too much; it's far better to get a small dose of asphyxia than a great big one of rigor mortis.

Controlled ascents have been made safely from depths in excess of 600 feet . . . without breathing aparatus!

If there is a sensation of fullness behind the breastbone or a feeling of lung overexpansion, exhale harder! A good rule of thumb is to stay behind your small exhaust bubbles on ascent.

Again, knowing the location of the nearest recompression chamber and the fastest route there should be an important pre-dive preparation.

There are several other possible consequences of lung damage caused by ascending while holding the breath. They are far less serious, but worthy of discussion.

PNEUMOTHORAX

Like air embolism, pneumothorax is caused by the overexpansion and rupturing of the lung alveoli. However, no air bubbles enter the blood stream. Instead, rupture of the lung surface occurs through a weakened area (medically known as a bleb) and air enters the space between the lungs and the lining of the chest wall. Generally, severe and sharp chest pain occurs and breathing is somewhat short. On further ascent, the expanding air will collapse the affected lung and force the lung and heart to the other side of the chest impairing both the action of the heart and the normal breathing cycle. The victim may become cyanotic, although this is not a reliable sign.

TREATMENT

The trapped air in the pleural cavity must be removed by a physician. This is accomplished by the insertion of a syringe or needle through the chest wall into the air pocket, relieving that pressure, and reinflating the lung. Unlike air embolism, recompression is of little value.

MEDIASTINAL EMPHYSEMA

Air from the ruptured alveoli may travel along the bronchi and enter the tissue spaces in the mediastinum *(center of chest)*. The victim may experience a sensation of fullness in the chest with difficulty in breathing. A mediastinal "crunch" may be heard above the heartbeat.

In a severe case, recompression is definitely advisable. No active medical treatment *(other than for shock)* is generally required.

SUBCUTANEOUS EMPHYSEMA

Oftentimes associated with the mediastinal emphysema, the air from the mediastinum will travel upwards into the neck, gathering under the skin, and causing the neck to swell like a collar. This is not a serious condition and the air will be dissipated through the body, although a crackling noise produced by the stretched skin around the swollen neck can be somewhat unnerving.

PREVENTION

As indicated in the section on air embolism, never hold your breath while using scuba equipment. Breathe normally on ascent.

DIVER'S COLIC

Occasionally, scuba divers will develop some excess gas in the stomach and intestine. This is particularly true, where the neophyte diver performs the Valsalva maneuver *(ear popping)* a bit too enthusiastically and swallows air. It may also occur because of eating beans, or cabbage or other gas-forming foods prior to the dive.

Upon ascent, the resulting gas may expand, overfilling the intestine and possibly causing abdominal cramps. Generally, the diver's colic is easily remedied by either belching or other natural means of relieving excess stomach gas.

PREVENTION

Care should be taken in ear clearing exercises to prevent swallowed air. Divers are advised to eat sensibly before dives, avoiding spicy foods and carbonated beverages.

QUESTIONS ON CHAPTER 7

1. Explain the importance of Henry's Law in diving.
2. Describe (step by step) how decompression sickness occurs.
3. How does a diver prevent decompression sickness?
4. Define the term "bottom time".
5. What is a repetitive dive? Why is it important to understand the repetitive dive tables?
6. What is the treatment for a diver stricken with decompression sickness?
7. Describe (step by step) how an air embolism occurs.
8. How is an air embolism prevented?
9. What are the basic differences between air embolism and decompression sickness?
10. Compute the decompression time and stops (if any) of the following dives:

| | 1st Dive | | | 2nd Dive | |
| | | | | | |
Depth (ft.)	Bottom Time (min.)	Surface Interval (min.)		Depth (ft.)	Bottom Time (min.)
A. 150	40	....			
B. 120	20	2 hrs. 30 min.		80	63
C. 105	18	3 hrs. 0 min.		45	60

"You all know as well as I do, Professor, that man can live underwater, providing he carries with him a sufficient supply of breathable air . . . it consists of a reservoir, in which I store air under a pressure of fifty atmospheres."

Captain Nemo, *"Twenty Thousand Leagues Under The Sea"*

Chapter 8   THE BUBBLE MACHINE

"Bubble machine" is a term of affection used to describe the open-circuit, demand scuba (*self contained underwater breathing apparatus*), which has been used safely since 1943 by over 10 million diving enthusiasts. The diver using the "bubble machine" draws pure compressed air from a high pressure cylinder and exhales completely into the surrounding water. No re-breathing or recirculation of the gases occurs. And only the open-circuit, demand scuba is considered safe for sport diving.

PRESSURE BALANCE

The diver cannot effectively expand and contract his lungs unless the air he is breathing is at a pressure equal to the surrounding water pressure.

Picture a diver only 18 inches below the surface of the water. If he tries to inhale atmospheric air through a snorkel, he will find that the added 18 inches of water pressure against his chest will prevent his lungs from expanding.

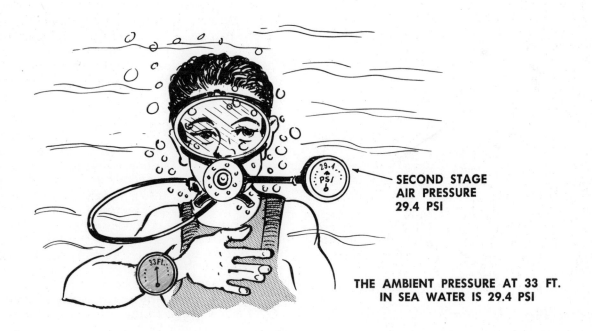

SECOND STAGE
AIR PRESSURE
29.4 PSI

THE AMBIENT PRESSURE AT 33 FT.
IN SEA WATER IS 29.4 PSI

The diver cannot effectively expand and contract his lungs unless the air he is breathing is at a pressure equal to the surrounding water pressure

The same diver at the surface would find it equally impossible to exhale through a snorkel immersed in 18 inches of water.

If the diver is to breathe comfortably underwater, the breathing apparatus must reduce the high pressure cylinder air to precisely balance the surrounding water pressure.

OPEN CIRCUIT DEMAND SCUBA

In this system, high pressure cylinder air is automatically reduced to balance the ambient pressure and released to the diver on demand (inhalation). Regardless of cylinder pressure, the flow of air is smooth and the volume is constant. The flow is not continuous, but controlled by the diver's breathing requirements. The heart of this system is the demand regulator.

DEMAND REGULATOR

The demand regulator is basically a pressure-reduction valve. It is a water-tight, rigid container with one flexible rubber side (diaphragm) exposed to the surrounding water pressure.

Inside the container is a high-pressure demand valve and a lever system designed to open the valve when depressed.

Since the flexible side (diaphragm) of the rigid container is exposed to the water pressure, an equal air pressure must be maintained inside the container if the diaphragm is to remain in a state of balance.

Anytime the internal pressure is reduced, the surrounding water pressure will deflect the diaphragm toward the lower pressure.

As the diver inhales, internal pressure is reduced and the diaphragm is deflected. The lever is depressed forcing the demand valve open and air is released to the diver.

The cylinder pressure is automatically reduced to equal the surrounding water pressure in either one or two stages depending upon the type of demand regulator.

The slightest inhalation will deflect the diaphragm sufficiently to start an air flow and maintain it as long as the diver continues to inhale.

AIR FLOW

Even the act of breathing requires greater effort as the diver goes progressively deeper. While the average diver uses about one cubic foot of air per minute doing light exercise at the sur-

face, that rate might be four times as high (4 cubic feet) doing moderate exercise.

Doing the same moderate exercise at a depth of 132 feet, the diver would demand as much as 20 cubic feet of air per minute!

The volume of the diver's lungs has not changed, but the molecules of air have been compressed into one fifth the space they occupied at the surface. As a result, the air the diver is pulling through the regulator orifice is five times as "thick" as atmospheric air.

If the regulator cannot quickly deliver these tremendous volumes, the extra breathing effort required will result in lung fatigue, a strain of the chest muscles. A chain reaction thereby results. The cylinder air is breathed at an abnormally high rate, metabolism goes up, and the diver is unfit for further work. Well designed regulators deliver the required volumes of air without increasing the breathing effort. Much of this effort is eliminated by incorporating a "venturi" in the demand regulator.

VENTURI

As the diver inhales, air jets through the venturi and creates a suction pressure in the air chamber. In effect, the diaphragm is held depressed by this suction pressure permitting a greater flow of air with less effort by the diver.

The diver breathes easier since he doesn't have to overcome the resistance of the diaphragm by lung effort alone. This feature is of particular importance at increasing depths where the air's greater density increases breathing resistance and corresponding lung fatigue.

SINGLE STAGE REGULATOR

Early models of the single stage regulator severely restricted the flow of adequate volumes of air with increasing depth and low cylinder pressure. However, through compound levering, larger orifices, and the venturi principle easier breathing has been provided, even as cylinder pressure decreases. In the single stage regulator, cylinder pressure is reduced to ambient pressure in one stage of pressure reduction. Since it contains only one valve mechanism, it has fewer parts and is consequently less expensive to manufacture as compared to the two stage regulator.

OPERATION

1. As the diver inhales, pressure in the air chamber under the rubber diaphragm is lowered.

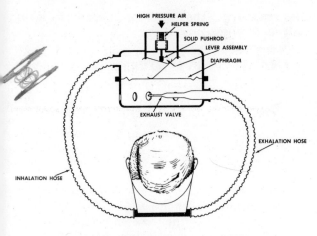

Single Stage Regulator — Balanced

2. The ambient water pressure depresses the flexible diaphragm to equalize the lower pressure.

3. As the diaphragm moves down, the pivoted lever assembly is depressed. In turn, the solid pushrod forces the valve seat open against the balancing spring. Cylinder pressure now flows through the small orifice into the air chamber and is reduced to the ambient pressure.

4. The air, now equalized with ambient pressure, is delivered to the diver while he continues to inhale.

5. Once his inhalation stops, the air flows into the air chamber until the pressure builds sufficiently to balance the surrounding water pressure. The diaphragm then returns to a neutral position.

6. When the diaphragm is balanced and the tension on the lever assembly and solid pushrod is relieved, the cylinder pressure and helper spring seat the high pressure valve—stopping the incoming flow of air.

7. The diver completes the breathing cycle by exhaling into the mouthpiece. His exhalation passes through the exhaust hose and non-return valve into the water. The regulator is now ready for the next breathing cycle.

TWO STAGE REGULATOR (TWO HOSE)

In this regulator, the cylinder pressure is reduced to the ambient pressure in two stages. In the first stage, cylinder pressure is reduced to about 120 p.s.i. *above* the surrounding water pressure. In the second stage, it is further reduced to balance the surrounding water pressure. The two stages are assembled in one housing which is attached to the cylinder valve.

FIRST STAGE OPERATION

1. Anytime the first stage pressure drops below 120 p.s.i. over ambient pressure, the first stage diaphragm will be deflected toward the lower pressure.

2. The action of the diaphragm is transmitted to a push rod which holds the high pressure seat open against the stream of incoming cylinder air. This cylinder air builds up the first stage pressure, forcing the first stage diaphragm to compress the high pressure spring.

3. The high pressure spring is factory-calibrated so that the high pressure valve closes when the first stage pressure reaches approximately 120 p.s.i. over ambient pressure.

4. The spring side of the high pressure diaphragm is also exposed to the second stage pressure, which always balances the surrounding

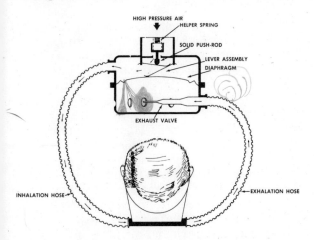

Single Stage Regulator — Open

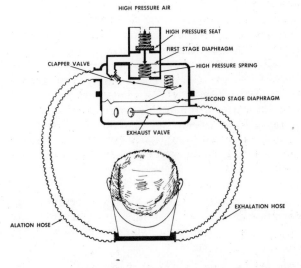

Two Stage Regulator (2 Hose) Balanced

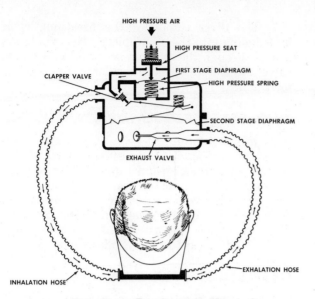

HIGH PRESSURE AIR

HIGH PRESSURE SEAT

FIRST STAGE DIAPHRAGM

CLAPPER VALVE

HIGH PRESSURE SPRING

SECOND STAGE DIAPHRAGM

EXHAUST VALVE

INHALATION HOSE

EXHALATION HOSE

Two Stage Regulator (2 Hose) Open

water pressure. As the surrounding water pressure increases, the pressure increase is transmitted to the high pressure diaphragm adding the increased ambient pressure to the 120 p.s.i. spring pressure. This insures that the first stage pressure reduction will always be 120 p.s.i. *over* the surrounding water pressure.

SECOND STAGE OPERATION

1. With the diver's slightest inhalation, the pressure is lowered under the large diaphragm. The ambient water pressure, separated from the air chamber by the diaphragm, depresses the flexible diaphragm to equalize the low pressure area.

2. The secondary lever is depressed by the diaphragm, and the clapper valve is, in turn, raised. Air flows into the second stage and to the diver.

3. When the diver stops inhaling, the air will continue to flow until the second stage pressure equalizes the ambient pressure and the diaphragm is returned to its balanced position.

4. As the diaphragm is balanced, the levered clapper valve closes and the pressure in the first stage increases until the high pressure valve is reseated.

5. The action of the two stages occurs simultaneously. The flow of high pressure air into the first stage precisely balances the flow of low pressure air to the diver.

6. The diver's exhalation passes out the exhaust hose into the water and the breathing cycle

is completed. The regulator is ready to supply air at the next inhalation.

EXHAUST VALVE LOCATION

We have already learned the importance of inhaling and exhaling air at a pressure equal to the surrounding water pressure.

In order that exhalation be as effortless as possible, the exhaust valve must be located at the center of the demand diaphragm to minimize any pressure differential.

Picture a diver wearing a two hose regulator who detaches the exhaust hose from the regulator housing and raises the loose end toward the surface. Regulator air will free flow toward the lower pressure until the cylinder empties or the diver lowers the hose to the level of the demand diaphragm. Conversely, lowering the free end of the exhaust hose below this level will again increase the pressure differential and the diver may not be able to exhale against the increased water pressure.

TWO STAGE REGULATOR (SINGLE HOSE)

In the single hose regulator the stages are not assembled together in one housing, but separated by a high-pressure hose. The first stage, reduces cylinder pressure to about 120 p.s.i. *above* the surrounding water pressure. This intermediate pressure is carried to the second stage, contained in the mouthpiece, by the high pressure hose. In the second stage, the intermediate pressure is further reduced to balance the surrounding water pressure.

FIRST STAGE OPERATION

(1) Anytime the pressure in the first stage *(including the high pressure hose)* drops below 120 p.s.i. over ambient pressure, the first stage diaphragm is deflected toward the lower pressure.

(2) This movement of the flexible diaphragm is transmitted to the stem valve which forces the high pressure seat open. High pressure cylinder air then flows into the first stage.

(3) The first stage diaphragm is exposed to water pressure in addition to the 120 p.s.i. spring. As a result, the high pressure valve will remain open until the pressure in the first stage equals 120 p.s.i. over ambient pressure.

(4) Thus, the cylinder air flows into the first stage until the pressure is sufficiently increased

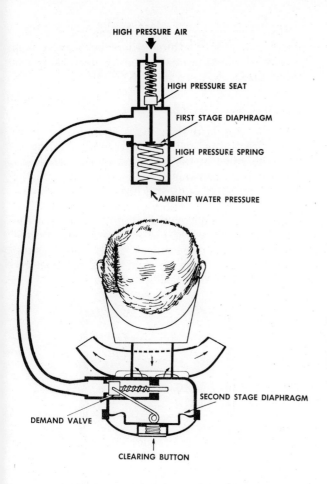

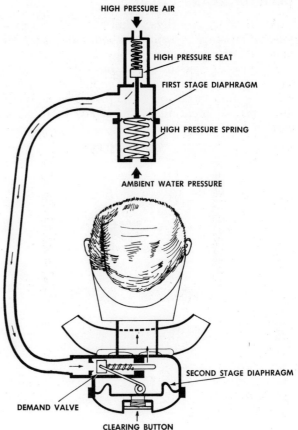

Two Stage Regulator (Single Hose) Balanced

Two Stage Regulator (Single Hose) Open

to compress the 120 p.s.i. spring and rebalance the diaphragm.

SECOND STAGE OPERATION

The second stage balances the water pressure outside the demand diaphragm with air pressure under the diaphragm. This insures that air delivered to the diver is equal to the pressure of the surrounding water.

1. The diver's slightest inhalation lowers the pressure under the second stage diaphragm. The water pressure forces the diaphragm toward the lower pressure.

2. The diaphragm depresses the demand valve lever and unseats the second stage valve. Air flows from the first stage as long as the diver inhales.

3. Once the diver's inhalation stops, the incoming air continues to flow until the second stage pressure equals the ambient pressure. The diaphragm is thus balanced, the valve reseated, and the air flow stops.

4. The diver's exhalation passes through the nonreturn valve in the mouthpiece into the water. The breathing cycle is completed and the regulator is ready for the next cycle.

STANDARD FIRST STAGE VALVE

Some mention should be made of the relative inefficiency of the standard first stage valve. As the cylinder pressure drops from 2,250 p.s.i. *(when the cylinder is fully charged)* the pressure of the first stage air changes correspondingly.

In the standard first stage, cylinder pressure either opens or closes the first stage valve. If the valve seat opens in the same direction as the air flow it is termed a *downstream* valve. Conversely, an *upstream valve* is one which opens *against* the flow of high pressure air. The valve spring is pre-set to hold the valve either open or closed against a fully charged cylinder.

DOWNSTREAM VALVE

At the start of a dive, a full cylinder will provide a first stage pressure of about 120 p.s.i. over ambient pressure.

As cylinder pressure drops, however, less pressure acts to open the valve. The first stage pressure may now be cut off at 80 p.s.i. over ambient pressure and breathing will become more difficult.

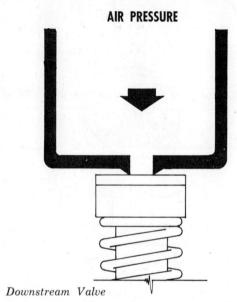

AIR PRESSURE

Downstream Valve

UPSTREAM VALVE

In contrast, the upstream valve opens against the flow of high pressure air. The spring tends to hold the valve open as cylinder pressure drops and the first stage pressure may increase to 160 p.s.i. As cylinder pressure drops, the pressure delivered to the second stage increases because there is less force closing the valve. Breathing becomes easier as cylinder pressure lowers.

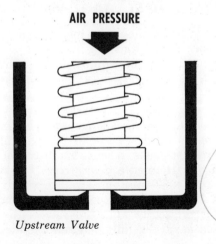

AIR PRESSURE

Upstream Valve

Since such changes in first stage pressure impair the diver's breathing efficiency, a valve was developed which is unaffected by decreasing cylinder pressure.

BALANCED VALVE

In the standard first stage, cylinder pressure flows directly against the valve end, tending to push the valve in the direction of the air flow.

In the balanced valve, the cylinder air is routed around the valve ends and has no effect in seating or opening the valve. Only the mechanical action of the diaphragm and springs control the operation of the valve and exact first stage pressure is maintained regardless of cylinder pressure.

Larger orifices can be used resulting in larger volumes of air and easier breathing.

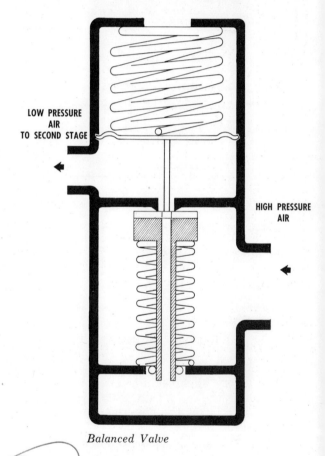

LOW PRESSURE
AIR
TO SECOND STAGE

HIGH PRESSURE
AIR

Balanced Valve

REGULATOR POSITIONING

The positioning of the demand regulator with respect to the diver's lungs is quite important. The breathing effort required to start the demand regulator depends upon the water pressure

Regulator Positioning

differential between the demand diaphragm and the center of the lungs. In the normal swimming attitude, the regulator is in its best position, when the center of the regulator is located between the diver's shoulder blades.

If a diver wearing a two hose regulator rolls over on his back, air will free flow into his mouthpiece. Lifting the mouthpiece as little as two or three inches above the regulator will cause a free flow. Two hose regulators are sensitive to the slightest pressure differential and when the mouthpiece is raised, air in the regulator flows toward the lower pressure in the mouthpiece.

The diver swimming face down will find that breathing is a bit harder because the pressure differentials are reversed. However, free flows theoretically will not occur in single hose regulators because the mouthpiece and demand diaphragm are assembled in close proximity. As a result no pressure differential can occur.

NON-RETURN VALVE

Incorporated in the regulator are non-return valves, which are one-way valves opening only in the direction of the air flow. Their function is to prevent water from entering the regulator or breathing hoses.

BACKPACKS AND HARNESS

Certainly the most comfortable rig in recent years is the body contoured back pack made of vinyl-coated aluminum. Many are equipped with self-locking cams for rapid tank changing and adjustable two inch wide nylon harness. The harness comes with quick-ditch shoulder snaps and quick release buckle on the waist strap.

Regardless of the type used, it should be snug fitting, comfortable and be equipped with quick release fastenings for jettisoning.

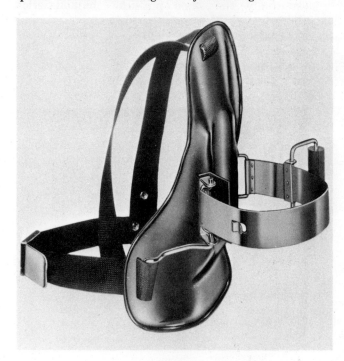

Scuba Backpack

COMPRESSED AIR TANKS

The standard 71.2 cubic foot air cylinder is designed to withstand great internal pressures. Such a cylinder when fully charged, would contain 71.2 cubic feet of air at a pressure of 2475 p.s.i. *(2250 p.s.i. plus a ten percent overcharge).* Although the actual volume of the tank is less than one half cubic foot, if the high pressure air were released to atmospheric air it would fill a 71.2 cubic foot area. Atmospheric air then is termed *"free"* or uncompressed air.

Normally, scuba cylinders are charged to the maximum rated pressure (2250 p.s.i.) providing a volume of only *64.6 cubic feet.*

These chrome-molybdenum tanks weigh approximately 35 pounds, and when fully charged, have the equivalent of one ton of force being exerted on every square inch of inside cylinder surface for a total of 433 tons of force.

ALUMINUM TANKS

One of the most exciting spin-offs of space-age technology to be implemented by the diving industry is the use of high strength, rust-free

63

aluminum (alloy 5361T6) in the manufacture of scuba tanks. Besides the obvious advantage of being rust proof, the new aluminum tanks have essentially the same physical characteristics (buoyancy, weight and size) as conventional steel tanks with one delightful exception . . . air capacity. The new aluminum tanks can be safely filled to a pressure as high as 3,000 p.s.i. with an air capacity to 80 cubic feet!

Non-Reserve Valve

Aluminum Tanks

CYLINDER VALVES

These are simply mechanical controls that regulate, start, and stop the flow of air from the cylinder to the demand regulator. Basically, there are two categories of valves: the non-reserve valve and the reserve valve.

NON-RESERVE VALVE (K)

This valve may be compared to the kitchen faucet in that it is simply an on-off valve, doing no more than releasing or stopping the flow of cylinder air.

Since it provides no "reserve" air, its use should be limited to water depths of 25 feet or less. It may be argued that at any depth, a volume of air remains in the cylinder at a pressure equal to the surrounding water. And if the diver ascends immediately, breathing shallowly, the decreasing ambient pressure will enable the calm diver to breathe this remaining volume safely to the surface. Although this is true, it does not constitute a safe reserve.

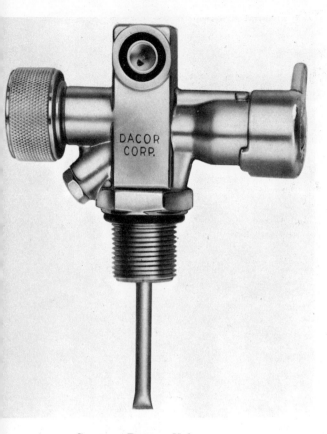

Constant Reserve Valve

CONSTANT RESERVE VALVE (J)

In the "J" reserve, a spring-loaded valve is held open by the cylinder pressure directed against it. When the cylinder pressure drops to approximately 300 p.s.i., the pre-set spring *(300*

p.s.i.) closes the valve against the cylinder pressure, restricting the flow of air to the diver.

The diver, alerted to his low air supply by the breathing resistance, pulls the reserve rod. This action mechanically retracts the spring-loaded valve and frees the remaining volume of cylinder pressure. Normal breathing is restored and the diver has adequate time to ascend safely to the surface.

In double tank units the spring is pre-set at 500 p.s.i. and in triple tank units, 750 p.s.i. The reserve valve actually closes off one tank while permitting the other tank(s) to be breathed dry.

When the reserve lever is pulled the reserve air pressure will equalize into the other tank(s) giving not 500 p.s.i. or 750 p.s.i. of reserve air, but 250 p.s.i.

And this is internal cylinder pressure, not pressure above the surrounding water pressure.

AUTOMATIC RESERVE VALVE (R) AND DEPTH COMPENSATED REGULATOR

Although no longer manufactured, the automatic reserve valve and depth compensated regulator are still around in sufficient quantities to merit some mention.

Both operate on the principle of the calibrated orifice. Inserted behind the high pressure inlet of the regulator and in the "R" valve body is a metal disc with a carefully sized orifice.

The calibrated orifice passes sufficient air to satisfy the diver's requirements as long as the cylinder pressure is relatively high.

However, once the cylinder pressure drops to a predetermined pressure *(generally about 300*

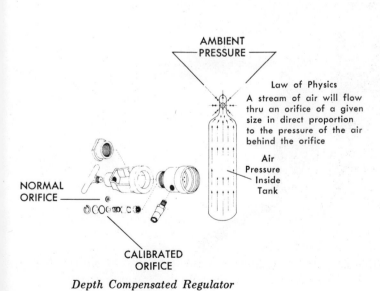

Depth Compensated Regulator

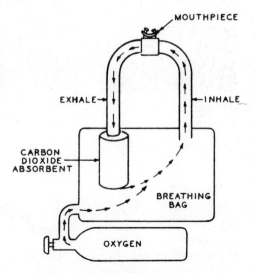

Closed Circuit Rebreather

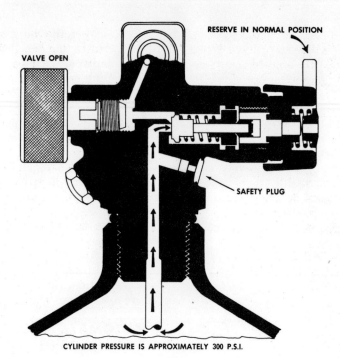

VALVE OPEN

RESERVE IN NORMAL POSITION

SAFETY PLUG

CYLINDER PRESSURE IS APPROXIMATELY 300 P.S.I.

Reserve in Normal Position

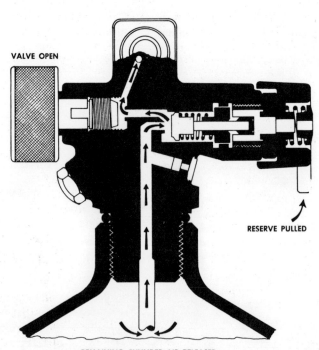

VALVE OPEN

RESERVE PULLED

REMAINING CYLINDER AIR RELEASED

Reserve Activated

p.s.i. above surrounding water pressure) less air will pass through the orifice in a given time.

This restricts the diver's breathing and he is warned of his low air supply. The diver must ascend immediately and the reduced ambient pressure will permit breathable volumes of air to pass from the cylinder. The kicker is that once the restriction begins, the diver *must* ascend immediately. Since this restriction is built into the depth-compensated regulator, there is no way to over-ride or bypass the calibrated orifice.

There are certain types of dives *(cave dives, wreck dives, for example)* which would preclude immediate ascents. The consequences are obvious.

The automatic reserve valves, at least, have bypass mechanisms with which the diver can free the remaining volume of air.

"BREATHING PAST" RESTRICTION

A diver breathing lightly in shallow water could breathe virtually all the available cylinder air through the calibrated orifice without being aware of any restrictions. If he were to descend rapidly and bypass the reserve expecting to free the remaining volume, he would discover there was no reserve air.

THE NON-BUBBLE MACHINE

The oxygen rebreather *(closed circuit scuba)* differs from the open circuit scuba in many ways. Most important, the breathing gas is pure oxygen and not air. This oxygen is alternately breathed, purified, and rebreathed. This continuous cycle efficiently utilizes the oxygen and allows no gas to escape into the surrounding water.

The unit consists basically of a *breathing bag* from which the diver breathes the pure oxygen, a canister of chemical absorbent *(which scrubs the diver's exhalation of all carbon dioxide)*, and a high-pressure cylinder of oxygen.

Unfortunately, this equipment has little value to the sport diver since its use requires extensive specialized training and even then its improper functioning may lead to highly dangerous situations. Since it emits no bubbles, the closed-circuit scuba does have a strategic value in military diving. However, this type apparatus is definitely taboo for the sport diving enthusiast.

INHERENT DANGERS

1) *Oxygen poisoning* is an ever-present possi-

bility and the use of the rebreather is limited by the U.S. Navy to a maximum depth of 25 feet.

2) *Carbon dioxide excess* may occur if the absorbent is inactivated through extended use or becoming water soaked. Improper filling of the canister may result in carbon dioxides channeling through the chemical absorbent.

3) *Hypoxia* is an insidious threat to the unsuspecting diver. It can occur when the diver, through negligence or ignorance, fails to purge the rebreather and his lungs of air. In effect, the unwanted air (80% nitrogen and 20% oxygen, approximately) in the breathing bag and diver's lungs would satisfy his oxygen requirements for only a minute or two. After the short supply of oxygen was exhausted, the diver would be rebreathing nitrogen. The sense of well-being that accompanys advanced hypoxia and the nitrogen expanding the diver's lungs would prevent his knowing anything was wrong.

FUTURISTIC SCUBA

A quarter century has ticked by since the invention of the open-circuit scuba, and technological refinements notwithstanding, the "bubble machine" has changed little in principle or efficiency. Diving depth and duration are still sharply restricted by low oxygen utilization.

The diver at best uses only 5% of the available oxygen in every cylinder of air. And this percentage decreases with increasing depth. Such inefficiency results from the complete discharge of each exhalation into the surrounding water. Underwater technology is ready for a breakthrough in advanced underwater breathing systems.

Some of the new concepts already under development are:
a) cryogenic scuba
b) artificial gill apparatus
c) semi-closed circuit scuba
d) computerized closed-circuit scuba

CRYOGENIC (LIQUID AIR) SCUBA

Would you believe a completely safe, open-circuit scuba that weighs only 15 pounds, yet has an air capacity adequate to satisfy any diver's breathing requirements for 12 hours? And on only *one air fill!*

Such a unit has already been test-dived over 1,000 hours and to depths in excess of 200 feet.

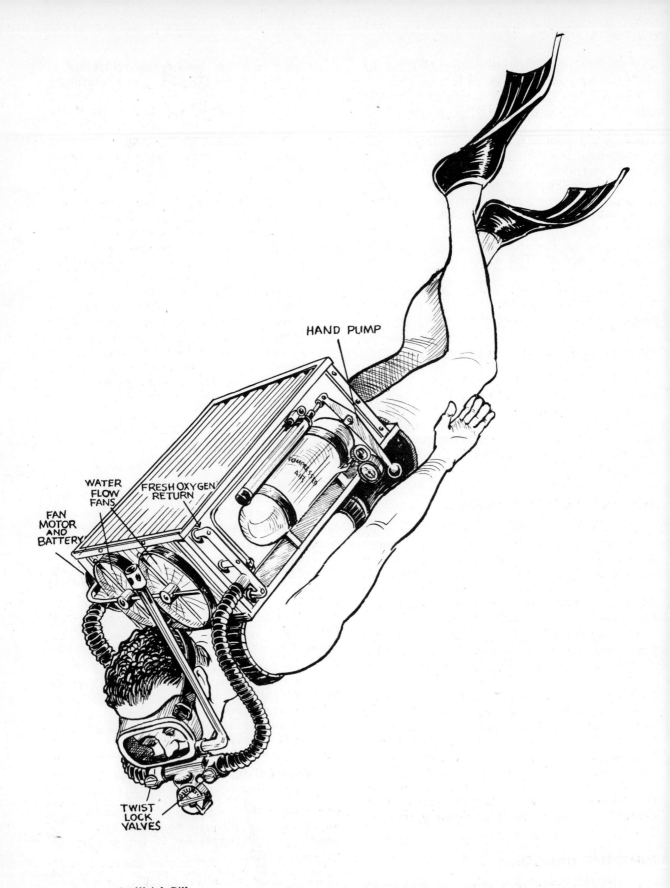

HAND PUMP

WATER
FLOW
FANS

FRESH OXYGEN
RETURN

FAN
MOTOR
AND
BATTERY

COMPRESSED
AIR

TWIST
LOCK
VALVES

Artificial Gill

Cryogenic scuba contains low pressure air in a supercooled *(—317.8 degrees F.)* liquified state. This complex apparatus must maintain this temperature in specially designed "thermos bottle" type cylinders. Keeping the liquified air well insulated and converting it to a warm breathable air mixture at a slow, even rate is an outstanding engineering achievement. Cryogenic scuba is truly the first of the futuristic scuba.

ARTIFICIAL GILL APPARATUS

The U.S. Patent Office has already awarded patents on two artificial gills which enable a free swimming diver to extract oxygen dissolved in sea water for his respiration. Carbon dioxide elimination is accomplished through the same device.

In effect, the artificial gill is a large *(100 square feet)* porous membrane. Through this membrane, oxygen from the water diffuses into the apparatus, while carbon dioxide from the diver's exhalation diffuses into the water.

Though this device has been successfully tested in shallow water, it does appear to have a definite depth limitation. Air in the apparatus is at atmospheric pressure. Gases dissolved in water are also at atmospheric pressure regardless of depth.

Since water pressure increases by .445 p.s.i. per foot of descent and the diver cannot tolerate any pressure differential between the water pressure and the air he is breathing, a significant obstacle temporarily blocks the development of this apparatus.

SEMI-CLOSED CIRCUIT APPARATUS

This type of apparatus is an important compromise between the high efficiency of oxygen utilization of the closed-circuit rebreather and the safety and the deep-diving capability of the open-circuit scuba.

Since the unit incorporates partial rebreathing and carbon dioxide scrubbing, oxygen utilization is vastly improved and time under water greatly extended. Generally, the efficiency of this apparatus is as much as ten times that of a comparable open-circuit unit at a depth of 100 feet.

A continuous flow of mixed gas through a constant mass-flow regulator into the rebreathing system provides a continuous purge of the breathing system preventing an unwanted buildup of any gas concentration—and possible hypoxia or oxygen poisoning.

Semi-Closed Scuba

ELECTRONICALLY REGULATED, CLOSED-CIRCUIT, MIXED GAS SCUBA

A step closer to the development of the "perfect deep diving scuba" is the "computerized, closed-circuit apparatus. The reader, after studying the preceding section which describes an apparatus *ten* times as efficient as open-circuit scuba, will probably be hard pressed to imagine a unit with *200* times the efficiency.

The system operates basically on the closed-circuit principle. However, the breathing mixture (tri-mix) combines oxygen, helium and compressed air. The helium and compressed air effectively dilute the oxygen to safe partial pressures and at the same time neutralize the inherent threat of nitrogen narcosis in deep, compressed-air dives.

Three oxygen sensing electrodes continuously monitor the partial pressure of oxygen in the mixture and transmit this data to a miniaturized computer. The oxygen needed to satisfy the diver's breathing requirements is determined by the computer and the precise amount is automatically injected into the system. Carbon diox-

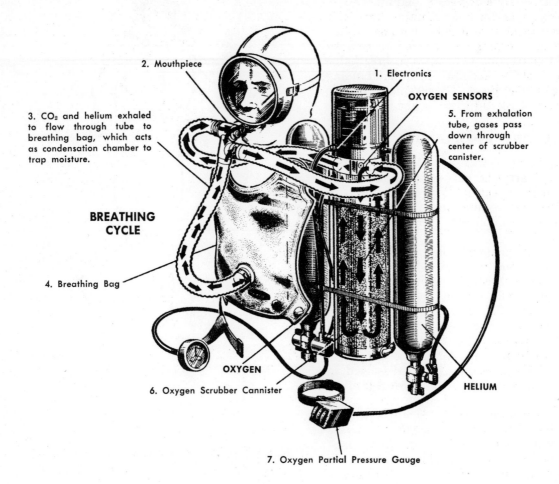

2. Mouthpiece

1. Electronics

OXYGEN SENSORS

3. CO₂ and helium exhaled to flow through tube to breathing bag, which acts as condensation chamber to trap moisture.

5. From exhalation tube, gases pass down through center of scrubber canister.

BREATHING CYCLE

4. Breathing Bag

OXYGEN

6. Oxygen Scrubber Cannister

HELIUM

7. Oxygen Partial Pressure Gauge

Computerized Closed Circuit Scuba

ide is absorbed continuously as the diver's exhalations circulate through a large cannister of baralyme.

There is sufficient evidence to indicate that the computerized closed-circuit, mixed gas scuba, when perfected, could open the vast frontiers of the Continental Shelf to the free diver by offering the greatest range of capability in diving.

QUESTIONS ON CHAPTER 8

1. Explain how the open-circuit, demand regulator supplies the diver with air at a pressure equal to the ambient pressure.
2. What is the difference between "single stage" and "two stage" regulators?
3. Why does a two hose regulator "free flow" underwater when the mouthpiece is raised above the regulator?
4. Describe the operation of: a) the downstream valve b) the upstream valve c) the balanced valve.
5. Why is the standard compressed air cylinder called a 71.2 cubic foot cylinder, when its actual volume is less than 0.5 cubic foot?
6. Explain the differences between the "J" valve and "K" valve.
7. Describe the principle of operation of the automatic reserve "R" valve.
8. Define the term "breathing past".
9. What is the basic difference between the "open circuit" and "closed circuit" scuba?
10. Explain the operation of electronically regulated, mixed gas, closed-circuit scuba.

". . . Relax! I told myself. If you don't, you've had it. Forget that it's hard to breathe. It's not pressure that's bothering you; it's not lack of oxygen; it's plain bloody panic. Just take it easy and save yourself. . ."

Peter Keeble, *"Ordeal By Water"*

Chapter 9   UNDERWATER SAFETY

There is a sign which hangs over the entrance to the famous underwater physiology laboratory of Siebe, Gorman & Co. Ltd., of London. It summarizes in a few words what diving safety is all about.

"There are old divers, and
there are bold divers . . .
But there ain't no
old, bold divers."

Occasionally some idiot, with a consuming need to impress people by defying all rules of good sense, discovers sport diving. His need to prove manhood and courage by flinging himself into the face of danger often ends with his being headlined as "another diving fatality".

And even more unfortunate, the idiot sometimes involves an unsuspecting soul, whose misplaced trust may well cost him his life.

An opportunity to dive with the great underwater team of the TV's "Sea Hunt" provided an interesting contrast in underwater safety. Real professionals like Lamar Boren, Ricou Brouning, Courtney Brown, and Willie Meyers are so totally safety-minded, one can't help but be impressed by their thoroughness. In many cases, their underwater activity was dangerous — of necessity. Nobody would have watched the show if it hadn't an element of danger. But their attention to detail and careful planning demonstrate a most healthy respect for the environment. If these great underwater men are so safety-conscious, it seems reasonable that the sport-diver should plan his underwater activities every bit as carefully.

PANIC

Diving accidents occur *only* through faulty judgment, lack of training or failure to recognize the limits of equipment and diver. All these factors can be eliminated through competent instruction. The cause of most diving accidents is panic, the diver's number one enemy.

Panic has been defined as an ". . . unreasoning fear, robbing the individual of logical thought, and reducing him to instinctive acts."

The untrained diver may lose all control as a result of panic. The well-trained diver conversely applies the mental brakes, looks the situation over, and follows the emergency procedure in which he has been trained. He has remembered to *STOP AND THINK*.

FEAR vs. PANIC

The best divers are those having normal fear reactions. It's absolutely normal to become a little alarmed if you surface after a dive, faced with a five mile swim to shore because your boat has snapped its anchor and drifted away. In fact, it's a blessing. The resulting adrenalin speeds the heart action, more oxygen is pumped to the brain, and the diver gets a little boost just when he needs it most.

No emergency requires a split-second decision. Take a moment to look over the problem. Then, take corrective action. *STOP AND THINK!*

THE BUDDY SYSTEM

The most important safety procedure yet conceived is the buddy system. The buddies are a pair of divers operating as a unit with each buddy responsible for the other's safety. The selection of a diving buddy is perhaps the most important diving-related decision a sports diver can make. His choice of a diving buddy should be

Panic

a friend who shares his underwater interests. Equally important, he should be a well-trained diver who embodies all the requisites of a safe diver: discipline, judgment, attitude, fitness and watermanship. The cardinal rule of diving is *NEVER DIVE ALONE.*

Safety aside, the thrill and adventure of diving is best enjoyed when shared with another diver.

In an emergency, the buddy system minimizes problems that could be of grave consequence to the lone diver.

When diving, keep your buddy in sight. Depending upon the visibility, buddies should never be more than 25 feet apart. The buddies should prearrange to surface immediately if they become separated. Following this procedure assures the team's regrouping quickly.

In very poor visibility, the divers should use a *buddy line*, a nylon line about 6 feet long. Each diver wraps an end around his hand and never, under any cirmustances, ties the line to himself or his equipment.

"OCTOPUS" REGULATOR

The good diver, it is said, never forgets his five "P's". *Prior Planning Prevents Poor Performance!*

Octopus Regulator

74

Emergency Swimming Ascent

The Buddy System

Prior planning, of course, begins with considerable thought given to contingencies. And one of the most important is what do you do if your buddy runs out of air? One answer to the problem is gaining widespread popularity — the octopus regulator.

The octopus regulator is essentially a single hose regulator (although some two hose regulators have been successfully converted to octopus configuration) which has an extra low pressure port to which an additional second stage is fitted.

The auxiliary mouthpiece can be held out of the way by neckstrap or attached to the shoulder harness by quick release snap. In the event of an underwater emergency, its worth is obvious. The octopus regulator is recommended for all but the most casual diving excursions.

EMERGENCY SWIMMING ASCENT

In the unlikely event of an equipment malfunction or the far more likely possibility of running out of air, the diver should signal his buddy and buddy-breathe to the surface. Let's say your buddy has wandered off and isn't aware of your plight. Even if your scuba were hopelessly fouled, you could extract yourself and reach the surface by using the following procedure:

A) Unless your scuba is impossibly entangled, do *not* ditch it. The emergency swimming ascent is a controlled ascent. Personal flotation device, buoyancy compensator and diving suit are normally "trimmed" for neutral buoyancy at depth. Ditching a weight belt — unless necessary — may result in enough added positive buoyancy to carry the diver to the surface in an uncontrolled ascent.

B) Tilt your head back, extend an arm over your head, exhale and begin swimming to the surface. As you ascend, the expanding air in your lungs *(Boyle's Law, again)* must be vented in a continuous exhalation. The head is tilted back to maintain a clear airway to the lungs.

C) If you feel a slight fullness in your chest, slow your ascent and blow harder. If you are blowing and seem to be running out of air, ascend a little faster.

PROCEDURE

The diver can survive afloat for days if he relaxes and keeps cool. A non-swimming victim of a shipwreck remained afloat without any floatation aids until rescued 38 hours later.

Your exposure suit *(wet or dry)* will provide more bouyancy than you need. The key to water survival is to relax and let the water support you. Practice the following steps.

1. Take a deep breath and relax. Stop all body movement. You may sink a few inches but your increased bouyancy will support you on the surface.
2. When you need another breath, tread water for a moment and exhale. Take another breath and continue the cycle.

DROWNPROOFING

Despite all the nastiness discussed in the chapters on medical aspects, drowning is the prime cause of diving fatalities. The National Safety Council reports that drowning accounts for one of every fourteen of all accidental deaths. Equipment failure is rarely a contributing factor. Panic and subsequent drowning may occur with sudden flooding of the untrained diver's mask. A drop of water falling through the nose and striking the glottis may cause a spasm and temporary inability to breathe. The trained diver simply swallows *(thereby unlocking the glottis)* and clears the water from the mask. The possibility of drowning can be eliminated through a healthy respect for the sea and strict adherence to the buddy system. No matter what the circumstances, the diver can survive if he only keeps his head.

Airway (Open and Closed)

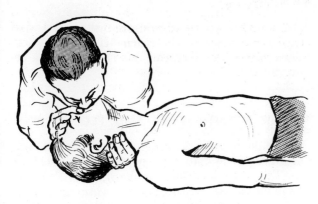

Mouth to Mouth Resuscitation

CARDIOPULMONARY RESUSCITATION

Recreational divers, for a number of reasons, probably have more opportunities to render life-saving assistance than any other group of sport enthusiasts. It stands to reason, therefore, that the diver prepare himself for such emergencies with the best information and training available. Without a doubt, the most exciting development in life-saving techniques is cardiopulmonary resuscitation (CPR) and every diver should be trained in its use.

CPR supersedes all previous life-saving techniques. It has been suggested most of the almost 700,000 Americans who die annually of heart attack might be saved thru CPR and hospital coronary care. CPR can be implemented in any case of sudden, unexpected death where heartbeat and breathing have stopped.

Cardiopulmonary resuscitation is really as basic as:

Airway
Breathing
Cardiac Compression

Remember: Begin immediately! Every second of delay reduces the victim's chances of recovery.

A for Airway

1) Place the victim on his back and quickly remove any foreign matter from his mouth and throat with your fingers.

2) Cup one hand under the victim's neck and lift. Place the other hand on his forehead and tilt the head backwards. In this way, a clear airway is opened to the lungs. Many times, through this simple act, the victim's breathing will be immediately restored.

B For Breathing

If breathing is not restored spontaneously, rescue breathing (mouth-to-mouth or mouth-to-nose) must begin at once.

1) While holding the victim's head in the open airway position, pinch his nostrils together. Take a deep breath and cover the victim's mouth tightly to form an airtight seal with your own. Blow until you see his chest rise.

2) Remove your mouth from the victim's and allow him to exhale passively. This cycle should be repeated about 12 times per minute (once every five seconds) for adults.

The rescuer can determine if adequate ventilation is taking place by:

1) Observing the rise and fall of the victim's chest

2) hearing and feeling victim's exhalations

3) feeling (in his own airway) the resistance and expansion of the victim's lungs.

The breathing cycle should be increased to about 20 to 30 cycles per minute for children. For infants, the rescuer must cover mouth and nose with his own mouth and puff gently to prevent overinflating the infant's lungs.

If a child's airway is obstructed by foreign matter; turn him over your arm; strike a sharp blow between his shoulder blades; and resume resuscitation.

The initial rescue breathing cycle should be done four times in quick succession. If breathing is not immediately restored, begin external cardiac compression at once.

C For Cardiac Compression

Earlier, under the heading CAROTID ARTERY CONSTRICTION, the location of the carotid pulse was described. CPR trainees should practice locating and feeling the carotid pulse until it becomes second nature. Heart stoppage is easily recognized by lack of carotid pulse, lack of breathing, and dilated (widened) pupils.

In the presence of these danger signs, the

rescuer must assist the heart in moving the blood to the brain and other vital organs.

1) The victim is already on his back, but he must be lying horizontally on a hard surface in order for the effective compression of the heart against the spine and a blood flow to the brain.

2) The rescuer kneels close to the victim's side and places the heel of one hand on the lower half of his sternum (breast bone) directly above the heart. The proper placement is determined by locating the lower tip of the sternum and positioning the hand 1 to 1½ inches above it.

To squeeze the heart enough to push blood to the brain, the lower sternum must be depressed about 1½ to 2 inches.

3) The free hand is placed on top of the other and with arms held straight, the rescuer exerts a downward pressure (as close to straight downward as possible). The pressure is immediately relaxed to allow the heart to refill. When only one rescuer is present, the ratio is 15 heart compressions to 2 very rapid rescue breaths. With two rescuers, (one doing the rescue breathing while the other administers cardiac compression)

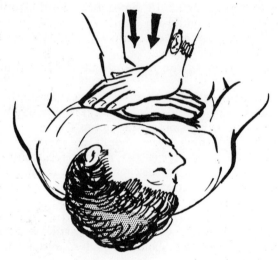

External Cardiac Compression

the ratio is one rescue breath to each 5 heart compressions. The compressions must be done at least once each second. The rescuer can determine if his efforts are successful by:

1) the return of normal skin color and

2) the victim's pupils growing smaller

CPR must be continued until medical assistance arrives and takes over.

It is notable that CPR has kept victims of

cardiac and respiratory arrest alive for over 4 hours with no trace of brain damage. And what achievement within the reach of man can be as rewarding as the restoring to another human being the gift of life.

DIVER DOWN FLAG AND FLOAT

The diver's flag, whether flying from the mast of a boat or mounted on an innertube towed by the diver, warns boats operating within the diving area that a diver is underwater and inside a 100 foot radius of the flag. Boats are thus warned to stay at least 100 feet away. In some states the diver is required by law to remain inside a 50 foot radius, theoretically insuring a 50 foot margin of safety.

The flag has an orange-red field measuring 4 units high by 4 units long. A white stripe, one unit wide, runs diagonally from the upper left to the lower right corners.

Even when flying the flag, the diver is advised to ascend cautiously. Although most boating enthusiasts respect the flag, some lunatic will occasionally try to use it as a racing pylon.

When operating off shore or away from his boat, the diver should tow a float with a diver's

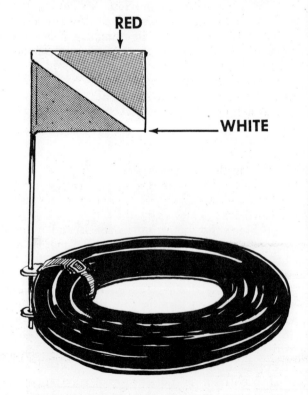

RED

WHITE

Diver Down Flag

Diver's Signal

flag mounted at least 3 feet above the water. An innertube makes an inexpensive carryall for the diver's equipment. In an emergency, it will support two fully-equipped divers.

DIVER'S SIGNALS

As explained earlier in the section on underwater physics, voice communications are all but impossible underwater. For the most part, hand signals can be successfully used between divers to communicate any vital message. In the rare event that complex messages must be communicated, the divers will find underwater slates and crayons bridge the gap nicely. The hand signals should be committed to memory and used.

SOUND SIGNALS

Divers may transmit sounds underwater by tapping on their high pressure cylinders with a knife or rock. This signal is used primarily to attract another diver's attention.

DIVERS WATCH

Among the "must have" accessories is the diver's watch. It is fundamental to the monitoring of bottom time, air consumption and the avoidance of decompression sickness. A good diving watch should feature: 1) a rugged case and shock-resistant movement; 2) a bezel ring (preferably click stop or self-locking) for tracking elapsed time; 3) a large, easy to read, luminous dial and hands; 4) water-resistant and pressure-tested to at least 600 feet.

Avoid the "cheapie"-type diving watches. They are at best unreliable and tend to become chronically waterlogged.

DEPTH GAUGE

Underwater safety requires that a reliable depth gauge be among the "must have" items in the diver's kit. The free-swimming scuba diver must have an accurate depth read-out continuously through his dive to avoid the problems of decompression and running out of air. Depth gauges are categorized by their principle of operation. *Capillary* gauges are the least expensive and correspondingly, the simplest. It is open at one end to ambient water pressure. As depth/pressure increases, water enters the tube which is calibrated in feet of water. Depth is read at the interface of the water column and the air pocket compressed inside the tube.

Diaphragm gauges consist basically of a pressure-sensing diaphragm and a geared movement. A large luminous pointer is linked to the movement and rotates about a dial calibrated in feet of water depth. The diaphragm may be in direct contact with the water or it may be separated from it by an oil-filled chamber. As depth/pressure increases the diaphragm is deflected, activating the geared movement which rotates the pointer about the calibrated dial.

Bourdon tube gauges utilize a coiled metal tube linked to a pointer which rotates about a calibrated dial. The pointer end of the tube is contained in a hermetically sealed case. Some Bourdon tubes are oil-filled and sense depth/pressure changes through a flexible diaphragm which caps the tube. Still others are sealed dry and encased in an oil-filled chamber. Changes in depth/pressure are transmitted through an air space which separates the oil-encased tube from the water with a pressure-sensing diaphragm. Under pressure, the coiled tube (like a collapsed balloon when inflated) uncoils ever so slightly thereby rotating the pointer.

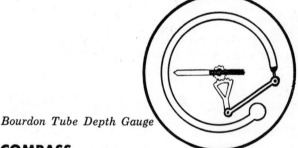
Bourdon Tube Depth Gauge

COMPASS

It has been suggested that there is only one sure-fire method to keep from getting lost underwater, and that is to stay found.

The diver's "staying found" is dependent upon a number of factors not the least of which is his possession of a reliable compass. There are any number of excellent compasses available to the recreational diver and he need only acquire one and learn to use it to increase his underwater enjoyment, save time and energy and return safely to his starting point.

A good underwater compass is above all accurate and easy to read. Degree markings and directional indicator should be luminous for navigation under low light conditions.

DECOMPRESSION METER

The decompression meter, in theory, is an instrument capable of simulating the rate at which human tissue absorbs or eliminates dissolved nitrogen. This device also monitors and memorizes the time and depth of dives — as well as the time spent at the surface between dives. In addition to collecting and storing this important data, the instrument calculates and indicates to the diver the precise times and depths necessary for decompression.

Surprisingly, a number of so-called automatic decompression computers have evolved during the last quarter century. Most were simply too expensive to survive in the diving market. Other, less sophisticated devices, have endured and gained wide acceptance. These use a porous ceramic filter element which is intended to represent a single critical human tissue. These "single tissue" meters do theoretically measure the amount of nitrogen absorbed and eliminated by the diver's body.

The most recent development in decompression computer technology is the *multi-tissue* decompression computer which is capable of more precisely simulating the body's uptake of nitrogen.

DISADVANTAGES

No mechanical device is fool-proof and the decompression meter is no exception. If abused,

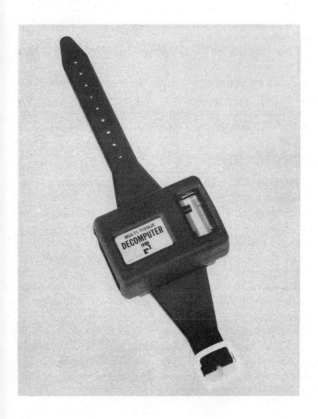

mistreated or neglected — there is no reason to expect that it will continue to give safe and accurate decompression data.

A number of decompression sickness cases have been reported which involved the use of meters. In many cases, it appears that the meters were incorrectly used. In others, the meters may have been damaged.

Although thousands of safe dives are made each year with the meter, it does — unfortunately — seem to invite a dangerous dependency.

SUMMARY

The concept of a decompression computer-type instrument is good. It is intended to be an aid to the diver — an adjunct to his ability to understand and use the dive tables and decompression procedure. It was never intended to be — and must never be considered — a short-cut or substitute. When carefully maintained and frequently checked for accuracy, it can be a most useful tool for the *avoidance* of decompression.

DIVER'S KNIFE

To the diver a knife is not a weapon, but an essential tool and in an emergency, a life-saver. It must be rugged and strong for it is used to hammer and chop, to pry and to dig; and even on occasion, to cut.

A good knife will have a saw-tooth edge on one side of the blade to saw through entanglements. It may be a floating or non-floating type as you prefer, although the non-floating type is generally more ruggedly constructed.

Most divers prefer to wear the knife strapped to the leg or thigh rather than on a belt.

GLOVES

Inexpensive work gloves will protect the divers hands from sharp coral, fire coral, and are strongly recommended when diving for lobster.

PERSONAL FLOTATION DEVICE

The personal flotation device is at the same time perhaps the best and the worst development evolved in recent diving technology. The best in that when properly maintained and used, the rubberized-nylon inflatable vest can adjust a diver's buoyancy, support a tired diver on the surface, lift objects from the sea floor and just possibly . . . may even save a life.

It is considered by a few as the worst because

in some cases it has induced a dependency among weak swimmers and suggested a margin of safety that permits them to overextend their physical capabilities. It is further argued that the personal flotation device suffers from chronic neglect in the hands of the average sport diver. As a consequence, there is little reason to expect it to function properly in the event of trouble.

In point of fact, the personal flotation device was never intended to be a self-rescue device (although it has been just that many, many times). It is in no way a substitute for watermanship and survival skills. It is instead a vital diving tool as fundamental to the recreational diver as his mask or fins. No good diver would consider going into the water without it. Color of the vest is largely a matter of personal preference. However, anyone who has ever had to search for a diver on the surface of a rough sea can appreciate the advantage of highly visible colors like bright yellow or international orange. The vest, when used for its intended purposes, simply makes diving safer, easier and vastly more pleasurable.

A good vest can be instantly inflated with a CO_2 cartridge triggered by a quick-acting pull release or it may be inflated orally.

Although safe buoyant ascents have been made from depths in excess of 600 feet, it is not advisable to fire the CO_2 cartridge underwater. *In shallow depths* (the area of greatest pressure change), a rapid, uncontrolled ascent could occur, with the possible result of serious lung over-expansion.

BUOYANCY COMPENSATOR

The most recent development in personal flotation device technology is the grouping of designs categorized as buoyancy compensators. These include the traditional vest-type design as well as the tank mounted pack-type compensator. The characteristic all have in common is the much larger bag size and consequently, larger air capacity than the conventional personal flotation device. Correspondingly, they provide the diver with greater buoyancy control.

Buoyancy compensators may be exclusively orally inflatable or exclusively scuba tank inflatable via hose and push button valve. Others offer the advantage of both oral and throw-away CO_2 cartridge(s) inflation. Still others incorporate a small refillable air supply instead of CO_2 cartridge.

Good buoyancy compensators integrate large vent valves in their design to minimize the threat of accidental over-inflation and subsequent loss of buoyancy control. Some models also include automatic inflators which are connected via quick-disconnect to the scuba regulator.

Whichever device you choose to use, it ideally should be both orally and CO_2 or air cylinder inflatable.

One particular nuisance common to some is the annoying trait of riding up around the diver's neck when inflated. Proper harness arrangement or crotch straps correct this problem. If your vest has this tendency, wear the waist strap *under* the beaver tail of your wet suit jacket.

MAINTENANCE

In order for the personal flotation device or buoyancy compensator to function as intended in an emergency, some careful maintenance is in order.

Before the dive:

1) Fully inflate the vest orally to insure air tight integrity and check oral inflation valve. Submerge to test for tell-tale bubbles leaking from vest or firing mechanism.

2) Examine carefully for any rips or weak spots on the vest or straps. Check the nylon pull cord for wear. If in doubtful condition, replace it. Remove the CO_2 cylinder and activate firing mechanism several times. If it is corroded, spray with WD-40 and clean.

Orally Inflating the Buoyancy Compensator Underwater

3) While the CO_2 cartridge is out, check that it hasn't been punctured. If it has been expended, discard it immediately to avoid inadvertently reinserting it in the vest. Carry a spare cartridge in your vest pocket (if it can be fastened) or in your gear bag.

During the dive:

Occasionally, the CO_2 cylinder should be test fired if only to insure the vest's proper operation as well as its ability to support the diver and his equipment comfortably on the surface.

After the dive:

1) Inflate the vest orally to smooth out wrinkles where pockets of water might accumulate. Thoroughly rinse the vest and firing mechanism with fresh water. Don't hurry the job!

2) When the vest has air-dried, deflate fully, fold and pack *carefully*.

3) Back home, lubricate all moving metal parts with silicone grease.

4) Support vest on an inflatable-type hanger and store in a cool, dry place.

5) When the oral inflation tube has been used underwater, it is likely that some water will get inside the vest. When used in corrosive salt water, it is particularly important to rinse the vest *internally* with warm, fresh water.

UNDERWATER AIR PRESSURE GAUGE

The underwater air pressure gauge enables the diver to monitor his tank pressure continuously while underwater. The gauge indicates the exact remaining cylinder pressure in p.s.i. The diver can quickly calculate the remaining volume *(cubic feet)* of air by multiplying the pressure reading *(p.s.i.)* by .0288. For example, a diver at 66 feet with 1,000 p.s.i. in his tank would know he has only 28.8 cubic feet of air remaining.

A glance at his watch tells him he has been underwater for about nine minutes. If he started with a fully-charged cylinder, his breathing rate has been about 4 c.f.m. At this rate, his remaining 28.8 cubic feet will be exhausted in just 7.2 minutes! An underwater air pressure gauge is as important to the sport diver as his mask.

FIRST AID

While a comprehensive knowledge of first aid is of great value to a diver, it is beyond the scope of this book. The student-diver is advised to take advantage of the free classes provided by the Red Cross. It is in the diver's best interests to pursue such study so that he be properly

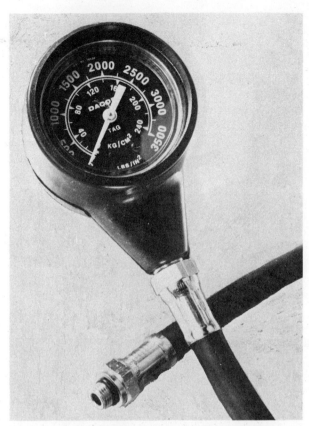

Underwater Air Pressure Gauge — The underwater air pressure gauge enables the diver to monitor his tank pressure continuously while underwater

trained to respond to any aquatic emergency. First aid is treatment performed by non-medical people before professional medical aid is available. It generally involves treatment given where:

a) The victim has stopped breathing.

b) The victim is bleeding.

c) The victim is in shock.

The primary responsibility of the rescuer is to restore breathing, an act which takes precedence over all other treatment.

Bleeding must be controlled and open wounds treated immediately. Where necessary, apply a tourniquet or a compression bandage. Once the hemorrhaging is stopped, treat the victim for shock by: restoring body heat, elevating his feet, and, if he is conscious, giving him hot drinks.

FIRST AID KIT

A complete first aid kit should be carried on all dives. Military surplus ammunition cases make excellent, water-tight containers. The fol-

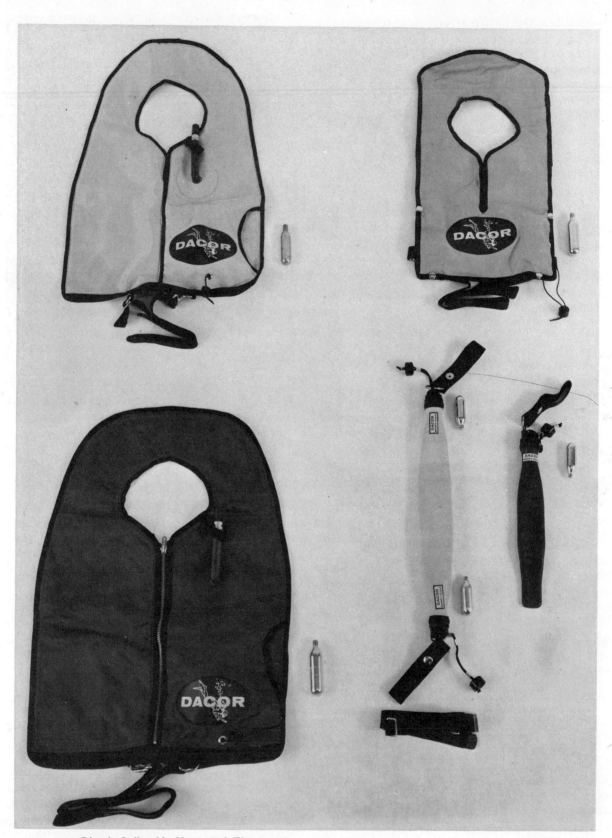

Diver's Inflatable Vests and Floats

lowing items comprise a good first aid kit:

WHITE SOAP, SMALL BAR
STERILE COTTON
SCISSORS
3″ TWEEZERS
TOURNIQUET
RAZOR BLADES, SINGLE EDGE
PAPER CUPS
SUNBURN OINTMENT
ANESTHETIC OINTMENT
CORTISONE OINTMENT
ANTIHISTAMINE OINTMENT
TINCTURE OF ZEPHIRAN
DILUTED AMMONIA
ADHESIVE TAPE, WIDE
BAND AIDS, ASSORTED
STERILE GAUZE SQUARES, (4″ x 4″)
GAUZE ROLLER BANDAGES (1″ and 2″)
STERILE COMPRESSION BANDAGES,
   ASSORTED
90% ALCOHOL EAR RINSE

ADVANCED DIVING ACTIVITIES

NIGHT DIVING

Although not recommended for the novice diver, night diving can be a highly rewarding experience for the seasoned diver when carefully

Underwater Light

planned and safely supervised. All forms of marine life are somewhat inhibited during the hours of daylight. But under the cover of darkness, the reefs come alive. The sea animals are hypnotized by the diver's light and fish that are skittish and elusive in daylight, become docile and even submit to being handled by the diver at night.

At the same time, the normal hazards of daytime diving are increased at night. The predatory fish move more boldly at night prowling the reef for food.

All the daylight rules for safe diving apply at night as well. In addition, the following are of particular importance when diving at night.

1) An *underwater light* is an essential bit of equipment for every diver in the group. The light, preferably a seal-beam powered by a 6 volt battery, should be affixed to the diver by a lanyard which can be slipped over the wrist preventing its loss and freeing the diver's hands.

2) *Buddy lines*, should be used between divers when visibility is limited. Once again group diving, when properly organized, is safer and more comfortable.

3) *Dive only in familiar waters* when attempt-

Night Diving

ing night dives. Water conditions should be examined during daylight on the day of the night dive. The safest dives are made from boats anchored over well-known reefs.

WRECK DIVING

No other underwater activity can evoke the sense of challenge or pure excitement as does diving on the wrecks of once proud ships.

It has been estimated that over 1,800 ships lie wrecked in the waters of the Florida Keys alone. An inestimable number of ships, many of which lie within the sport diver's depth range, have been wrecked in each of the Great Lakes. While this is diving at its exciting best, it is not without an element of risk.

1) Modern ship wrecks are often cluttered with sharp cables, broken glass, twisted pipes and torn metal which present a special hazard to the diver. Serious cuts or other injuries may be deceptively painless when the diver has been numbed by cold water. Be particularly careful when diving in and around wrecks. If cut or otherwise injured, surface immediately; and examine and treat the wound.

2) When entering a wreck through a hatch, the wise diver will tie the hatch open to prevent its accidentally closing, perhaps even trapping the diver inside. A safety line should always be used when probing inside a wreck. To retrace their steps, the divers need only rewind the safety line.

3) Wrecks are rarely to be found in clear water. In the usual shroud of poor visibility that covers a wreck, the diver must move cautiously since cables, pipes, and wreckage may entangle him. In the dark interiors of a wreck, the diver will need a light. He must avoid kicking up the bottom since the light will be of little value if the water is loaded with free-floating silt.

4) Ship's compartments should be entered cautiously. Wrecks occasionally settle on the bottom at some degree of list. Heavy furniture or equipment is often supported by the water in an unusual state of balance. Even bubbles from a diver's exhaust may be enough to upset this delicate balance. Heavy objects have been known to skid across a sloping deck, injuring or trapping a diver.

ICE DIVING

Unlike his brothers in the sunny south who are free to dive the year around, the snow bird in the frigid north has but two choices when winter winds begin to howl. He can either rack up his diving gear until the early spring, or he can break out the ice chopper and go diving.

Ice diving need not be the dangerous bug-a-boo it is often portrayed. When carefully planned and properly supervised, it can be a highly exhilarating experience. The land-locked diver will never see better visibility in his local waters for when the sun is high and the ice swept clear of snow, visibility in unparalleled.

There are a few special safety rules which must be closely observed.

1) A strong, highly visible *safety line* is an absolute essential. One end should be securely fastened to a large, stationary object, preferably ashore. The diving team should tie the free end of this line to themselves, allowing about 10 feet of line between each diver. The line is tied around the waist, allowing enough slack to take a turn or two around one hand. A surface tender should pay out and retrieve the safety line as the divers swim beneath the ice.

2) A fully-geared diver should remain at the surface ready to enter the water in the event of an emergency. His safety line should be at least 100 feet longer than the lines of the other divers. If a diver is lost, the safety diver swims out under the ice to the full length of his safety line, stretching it taut. He then swims a 360 degree sweep, dragging the tight line across the underside of the ice.

3) If a diver should lose his safety line, he should descend slowly, feet first, and scan the surface. Rotating slowly, he can scan the ice through a 360 degree turn. This maneuver is impractical if underwater visibility is poor.

4) If this method fails, the lost diver should immediately surface under the ice and inflate his vest. To preserve his air supply he must remain calm and slow his breathing rate. As soon as his buddy surfaces alone, the safety diver will start his sweep and the lost diver will be caught by the line.

5) Inflatable vests, snorkles, and knives should be worn on ice dives. The inflated vest will support a diver effortlessly under the ice and conserve his vital air supply. A knife can be used to chop a small hole through thin ice and the snorkle pushed through the hole to breathe until rescue is completed.

REGULATOR "ICING"

When the compressed air in the scuba cylinder has a high moisture content, the demand regu-

Safety Diver's Range

lator used in extremely low temperatures may "ice-up". This occurs because: 1) the high pressure air, at near-freezing temperatures in the scuba cylinders flows into the low pressure area *(first stage)*. The effect of the expanding air as it passes through the orifice reduction causes a drop in air temperature, and 2) If the moisture content is sufficiently high, moisture droplets will form ice around the first stage orifice restricting or even stopping the dynamic flow of air.

CAVE DIVING

Underwater cave exploration is one of the most satisfying of the advanced diving activities. To the proponents of cave diving, for the most part dedicated speleologists, the risks are far outweighed by the scientific rewards. Recently, for example, diving spelunkers from Florida State University found ivory tusks and a number of bones deep within Florida's Wakulla Cave. These discoveries were later identified as the remains of a mastodon, a prehistoric mammoth that became extinct *thousands* of years ago.

The underwater spelunker abides by a schedule of safety procedures which would discourage all but the most dedicated of sport divers. Just a

few of the basic rules are included here.

1) In cave diving, a strong safety line is an indispensible piece of safety equipment. Many cave divers prefer the reel type of rig which is securely fixed to the diver and feeds out a nylon

Cave Diving

line smoothly on descent and must be reeled in on ascent. When paying out the safety line, be certain the line is not stretched over a sharp rock edge where it could be sawed through.

2) As in ice diving, a standby diver should be stationed at the mouth of the cave, ready to go to the assistance of the diving team if for any reason communications through the life line are broken off.

3) Rugged, underwater lights are to be carried by each diver. Fresh batteries should be installed before every dive. When cave diving, underwater watches, depth gauges and cylinder pressure gauges are essential pieces of safety equipment. Bottom times must be carefully calculated and observed if decompression accidents are to be avoided.

Be alert for potential trouble spots: cave-ins or rock slides which may be set off by tanks banging against the ceiling of a case.

4) Better yet, take advantage of the specialized cave diving courses offered through the National Association for Cave Diving. And never attempt cave diving except in the company of an experienced cave diver familiar with the particular cave system.

SCUBA MAINTENANCE

Modern diving equipment is rugged, well-engineered, and built of materials guaranteed to last a life time if properly maintained and periodically overhauled by a qualified serviceman. The secret to long life and continuous service lies in routine maintenance and sensible handling.

SCUBA CYLINDERS

Considering the tremendous pressures held in the scuba cylinder, the sport diver is handling a potential bomb. He must treat the cylinder with the same respect he would a live bomb. Deaths have resulted because of careless handling of high pressure cylinders.

HANDLING

1) The Department of Transportation regulates the manufacture and testing of all high pressure cylinders. Scuba cylinders are *required*

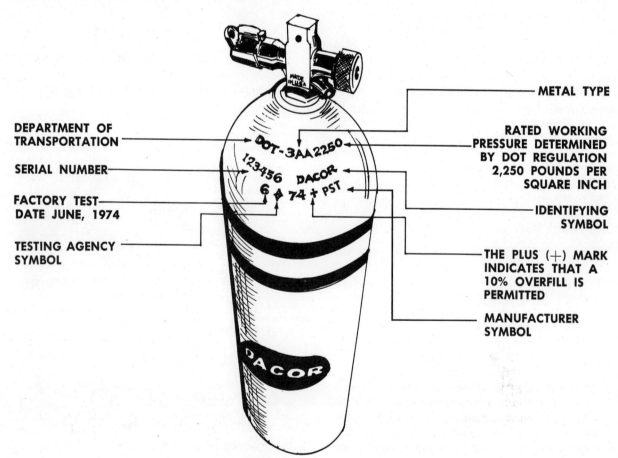

DEPARTMENT OF TRANSPORTATION

SERIAL NUMBER

FACTORY TEST DATE JUNE, 1974

TESTING AGENCY SYMBOL

METAL TYPE

RATED WORKING PRESSURE DETERMINED BY DOT REGULATION 2,250 POUNDS PER SQUARE INCH

IDENTIFYING SYMBOL

THE PLUS (+) MARK INDICATES THAT A 10% OVERFILL IS PERMITTED

MANUFACTURER SYMBOL

by the D.O.T. to be hydrostatically tested and recertified every five years. Sport divers are advised to have all scuba cylinders tested at least every three years and *any time* the cylinder is suspected to be damaged.

2) Scuba cylinders are to be filled only with pure compressed air. The D.O.T. rated working pressure for your scuba cylinder is stamped on the cylinder neck and must never be exceeded. The practice of overfilling places extreme stress on the cylinder walls and will result in a permanent weakening of the cylinder.

3) In addition to the pressure rating, the D.O.T. requires that every high pressure cylinder be stamped with a letter code identifying: 1) the type steel the cylinder is made of (*DOT3A would identify the material as a carbon or manganese steel alloy, or DOT3AA a chrom-moly or stainless alloy*), 2) serial number, 3) inspection mark, 4) owner or manufacturer's symbol (*registered with Bureau of Explosives*) and 5) hydrostatic test data.

4) Never weld, drill into or enlarge existing openings on high pressure cylinders. Always open the cylinder valve and release all pressure before working on a scuba cylinder. Never use oil or lubricant on any high pressure fitting, or allow charged cylinders to lie exposed to the rays of the sun.

5) Tie down, block, or otherwise fasten cylinders in transport to prevent front to back shifting or side roll. Position and pad the cylinders carefully so no heavy objects can be dropped on and damage either cylinder or valve.

STORING CYLINDERS

1) Scuba cylinders should be stored in an upright position. Should moisture collect inside the cylinder, corrosion will be far less detrimental on the cylinder bottom which is thicker than the cylinder walls. Never store a tank on end without fastening it to a wall. Even when standing in a rubber tank boot, it may be knocked over and the valve damaged.

2) Store cylinders with a pressure of about 100 p.s.i. to keep foreign material out. Tape the valve orifice with masking tape to prevent the loss of the rubber "O" ring.

DEMAND REGULATOR

1) The demand regulator as well as all other diving equipment, must be carefully rinsed in fresh water after use. Flush the mouthpiece and hoses several times and then shake vigorously to drain the water. Hang the regulator by the yoke to dry. Before rinsing, make certain the protective dust cap is tightened over the high pressure inlet.

2) The plastic dust cap should be snugged in place as soon as the regulator is removed from the scuba cylinder. Any particle of dirt inside the regulator may cause an air leak.

3) The sport diver's maintenance should be limited to hose, mouthpiece and exhaust valve replacements. Regulators should be cleaned and inspected annually by a certified serviceman or the manufacturer's repair department.

4) The cylinder valve "O" ring is absolutely necessary to provide a leak-proof seal between the cylinder and demand regulator. A wise diver carries several spare "O" rings on his regulator yoke screw as a contingency against its loss. Turn the yoke-screw out of the yoke, slide a few "O" rings over the threads, reinsert and tighten.

The preceding maintenance tips when carefully followed will extend the useful life of your diving equipment for years. Develop good maintenance habits now in the beginning of your diving career. You will be rewarded with many years of excellent service.

QUESTIONS ON CHAPTER 9

1. What is your first step should an emergency occur underwater?
2. Describe the differences between fear and panic.
3. Is the selection of a diving buddy important? Why?
4. Emergency swimming ascents have been made from depths greater than 600 feet. Explain the "emergency swimming ascent" procedure.
5. In diving, emphasis is placed on maintaining a relaxed pace underwater. What are the hazards of fast swimming or any heavy exertion?
6. Describe the most effective method of artificial respiration. What is the most important rule regarding its use?
7. Describe the diver down flag and explain its function.
8. Explain in detail all procedures and safety precautions you would employ in planning a wreck dive.
9. List several rules of special importance to night diving operations.
10. What agency regulates the testing of high pressure cylinders? When should a scuba cylinder be tested?

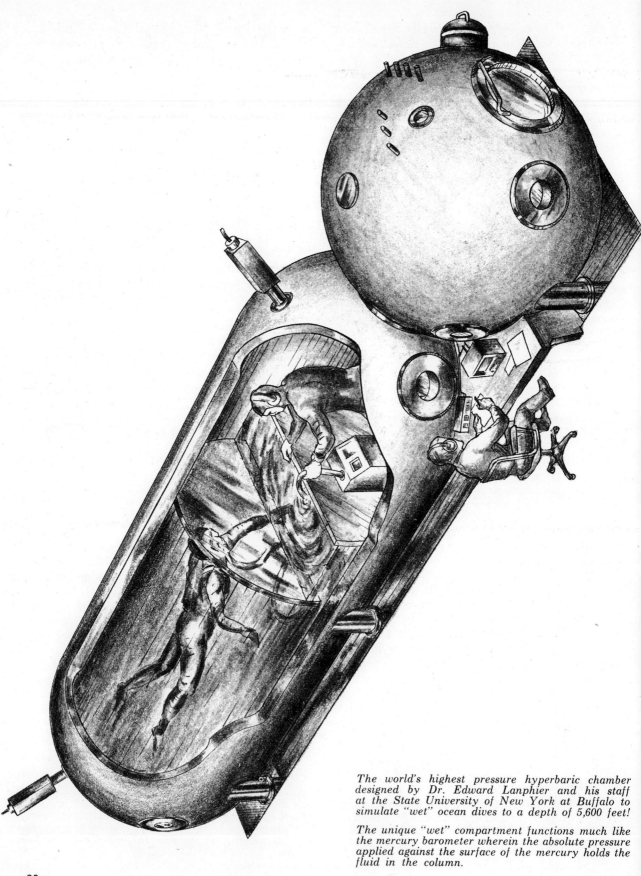

The world's highest pressure hyperbaric chamber designed by Dr. Edward Lanphier and his staff at the State University of New York at Buffalo to simulate "wet" ocean dives to a depth of 5,600 feet!

The unique "wet" compartment functions much like the mercury barometer wherein the absolute pressure applied against the surface of the mercury holds the fluid in the column.

"You are about to take a journey into wonderland. It is possible that your state of mind will be one of astonishment—nay, of stupefaction. You will find it hard to remain indifferent to the spectacle unrolling before your eyes."

Captain Nemo, *"Twenty Thousand Leagues Under The Sea"*

Chapter 10   YOUR FIRST DIVE

Your first dive, as any dive, should be carefully planned. Safe diving habits must be developed early if the diver is to enjoy the sport to its fullest measure. Planning a dive needn't be a time consuming drudgery, and once good habits are formed the procedures become almost instinctive.

RECOMPRESSION CHAMBER

It is the responsibility of every diver, whether he ever plans to make a decompression dive or not, to know the location of the operating recompression chambers nearest his area of diving activity. The wise diver also learns the fastest routes to these facilities.

Be sure that:
1) Patients will be accepted.
2) The chamber is ready for use.
3) Trained medical and operating personnel are available.

INTERNATIONAL CHAMBER LISTING

An international listing of recompression chambers has been compiled and published for possible emergency use by divers. Copies are available for $2.00 through NAUI Publications, 22809 Barton Road, Grand Terrace (Colton), California 92324.

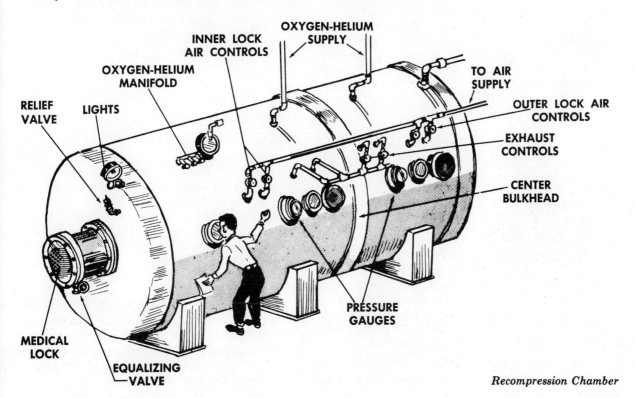

Recompression Chamber

Incidentally, the U. S. Navy is under no obligation to treat a civilian diver, and the availability of the above mentioned facilities is at the discretion of the Commanding Officer of the particular facility. The Navy is also empowered to exact a charge for treatment equal to its cost to the government. Moreover, the Federal District Attorney can enforce collection!

INTERNATIONAL RADIOTELEPHONE DISTRESS FREQUENCY

Whenever dives are being conducted from a sizable boat, the boat should be equipped with a radiotelephone. During diving operations Medium Frequency (MF) radios should be tuned to 2182 kc/s — the International Radiotelephone Distress Frequency. If a diver's life is in grave danger, transmitting a call on 2182 kc/s should bring assistance. The U. S. Coast Guard working frequency is 2670 kc/s.

CALCULATING RATE OF AIR CONSUMPTION

Before beginning the dive, the diver must determine if his air supply is adequate for the intended mission. Underwater time is governed by the depth of the dive, the diver's rate of air consumption, as well as the volume of free air compressed into the scuba cylinder.

The diver's approximate rate of air consumption is measured in cubic feet per minute (cfm) and it can be quickly calculated by using:

$$(\frac{D}{33} + 1) \text{ x } .75 = V$$

D = depth in feet
33 = feet of sea water equal to one atmosphere of pressure (34 feet in fresh water)
1 = additional atmosphere to convert to absolute pressure
$.75$ = hypothetical cfm of a diver doing light exercise at sea level. This figure may become four times as great with heavy exercise.
V = cfm at depth (D)

For example, the cfm at a depth of 66 feet

in sea water would be calculated:

$$(\frac{66}{33} + 1)\text{x}.75 = 2.25 \text{ cfm}$$

To calculate the duration (in minutes) of a scuba cylinder of a known volume, divide the available cubic feet by the computed cfm.

For example, calculate the duration of a 72 cubic foot cylinder.

$$\frac{72}{(\frac{66}{33} + 1)\text{X}.75 = 2.25 \text{ cfm}} = 32 \text{ minutes}$$

CALCULATING REMAINING VOLUME

To determine the actual volume of a partially charged cylinder:

$$\frac{P^2 \text{ x } V^1}{P^1} = V^2$$

P^1 = pressure of fully charged cylinder
P^2 = pressure gauge reading
V^1 = rated volume of cylinder at P^1
V^2 = volume of cylinder at P^2

For example, calculate the remaining volume of a 72 cubic foot cylinder when it registers only 1200 psi on a pressure gauge.

$$\frac{1200 \text{ x } 72}{2475} = \frac{86,400}{2475} = 34.8 \text{ cubic feet}$$

EQUIPMENT CHECKLIST

1) Always check cylinder pressure just before the dive. A pressure gauge will provide an accurate reading of high pressure air in your scuba cylinder. Begin each dive with a fully charged cylinder.
2) Be sure the constant reserve valve lever is working freely and in the "up" position. It is a good practice to check the valve's position during the dive to insure against accidentally pulling the reserve.
3) Check the scuba backpack to insure that the scuba cylinder is securely fastened and comfortably positioned so that the regulator cannot bang into the back of your head. Check the harness for tears, weak spots, and properly functioning quick releases. Adjust the harness for a comfortable fit.

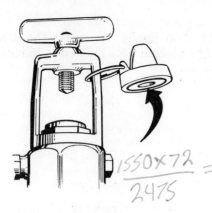

Spare "O" Ring

periodic physical examination by a physician conversant with the demands of sport diving will assure your physical qualifications.

2) Avoid the use of intoxicants for at least eight hours before the dive. Alcohol, medication, or sedatives may induce a dangerous loss of coordination and alertness.

4) Mount the regulator to the cylinder valve, carefully seating the regulator on the valve "O" ring. Tighten the yoke screw by *hand*. When properly mounted, there should be no air leakage. Check tightness of clamped connections on hose and mouthpiece assembly. Stretch corrugated hoses and inspect for cracks. Check carefully at the regulator horns.

5) Before opening the cylinder valve, inhale and exhale through the mouthpiece. If air flows into the mouthpiece, the equipment is defective and must not be used until the problem has been corrected.

6) Open the cylinder valve and listen for air leakage. Cylinder pressure tightens the regulator on the "O" ring, forming a high pressure seal. If there are no leaks, breathe with the unit several times to insure its proper operation.

7) When removing the regulator, turn off the cylinder valve and breathe or purge the remaining air from the regulator to break the high pressure seal. Now, the yoke screw may be loosened and the regulator removed.

PHYSICAL AND MENTAL FITNESS CHECKLIST

Equally as important as the condition of the diver's equipment, is the condition of the diver himself. Diving is a demanding sport. The diver, like the skiing enthusiast, should keep physically fit. And like the flyer, it is imperative to his safety that he be mentally fit.

1) Under no circumstances should you dive when suffering a cold, lung congestion, sinus obstruction or any respiratory discomfort. A

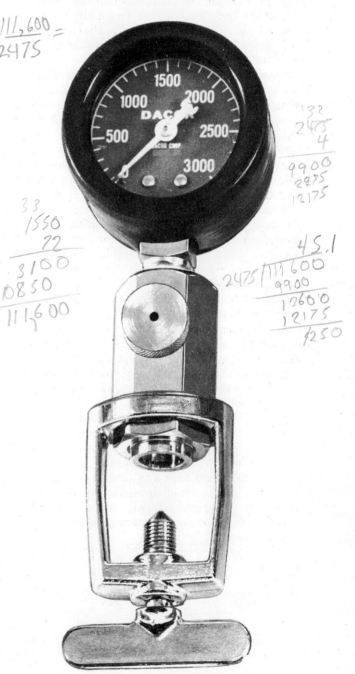

Cylinder Pressure Gauge

HYPOTHERMIA

There is strong evidence to support the theory that immersion in extremely cold water (30 degrees Fahrenheit) will cause death by hypothermia in as little as 90 seconds. Hypothermia can be defined as: the rapid, progressive mental and physical collapse that occurs when the temperature of the body's inner core (normally 99°F.) is lowered. It is significant to note that extremely cold water temperature is not a precondition to the onset of hypothermia.

Anytime the body loses heat faster than it can produce it, hypothermia occurs. And as a frame of reference, if the unprotected body is immersed in water at a temperature of 70°F., it will lose heat faster than it produces it.

At a theoretical compounded heat loss factor of about 25,000 times that of air, it is clear that unless the diver is adequately insulated from the cold water serious consequences will result.

Wearing a wet suit only delays the process and eventually the diver will become chilled. If the diver does not leave the water, the heat loss will continue with an inevitable drop in core temperature. In recent experiments, even well conditioned, highly motivated U.D.T. divers displayed symptoms of elevated heart rate, uncontrollable shivering, blurred vision and impaired ability to respond to tasks. After only a 3 degree temperature drop! Beyond this point, the effects range from increased air consumption, fatigue, progressive immobility to muscular rigidity, unconsciousness and failure of the cardiac and respiratory control centers.

One of the most frightening aspects of hypothermia is that as little as a 3 degree drop in core temperature will diminish the diver's reasoning power and judgement and he probably won't even realize that anything is wrong!

If he is not removed from the water and immediately rewarmed (ideally in a hot water 104°F bath), the rapid downward slide of core temperature will be fatal.

PREVENTION

1) Diving is for fun. Get plenty of *rest* before a dive. Diving when exhausted is simply stupid.
2) Eat plenty of high protein foods before a dive. When diving in cold water or during a surface interval between repetitive dives, nibble quickly-digested sweets.
3) Insulate yourself against the heat-robbing water. Wear a well-fitted wet suit as well as boots, gloves and hood when cold water diving.

4) And finally, terminate the dive at the first sign of chilling . . . before extensive heat loss occurs.

Dry Suit

DRY SUIT

For an idea of why an exposure suit is necessary in all but the most tropical of waters, one need only consider the fact that when diving, water carries away body heat by conduction at a rate 25 times faster than air. Furthermore, about 1,000 times more heat energy is required to heat a quantity of water to a given temperature as would be required by an identical quantity of air.

The dry suit is a watertight suit made of sheet rubber. Although the thin rubber has little insulating value itself, when an air space is created between the suit and the diver's skin by wearing thermal underwear, for example, the diver will remain reasonably warm in extremely cold water.

Because of this air space, the diver is compelled to offset substantial positive buoyancy with weights, often as much as 30 pounds.

If the dry suit leaks or is suddenly torn, this buoyancy is quickly lost and the diver may find himself becoming increasingly heavier in the water. The insulation as well depends upon the undergarments being kept dry.

Many dry suit devotees wear a ¼ inch wet suit under a dry suit incorporating the advantages of both in a warm but cumbersome combination.

WET SUIT

This type of exposure suit is the decided favorite of most sport divers. The wet suit is made of foam neoprene, a porous material containing literally millions of tiny air bubbles. This material is an excellent insulator because it places a barrier of air *(in the form of the air bubbles)* between the body and the surrounding water. The suit is not designed to be water tight and a thin layer of water may enter but it is quickly warmed to body temperature. The wet suit must be snugly tailored to the body if it is to be an effective insulator. Wet suits come in a wide range of thicknesses, *(1/8, 3/16, 1/4 and 3/8 inch)* and generally speaking, the thicker the warmer.

Tearing a wet suit underwater will result in little or no heat loss and since the buoyancy is in the material itself, no buoyancy changes occur. The foam neoprene is easily mended in minutes with neoprene adhesive.

In addition to its insulating properties, the wet suit is an excellent buoyancy aid. The air bubbles in the foam neoprene provide sufficient buoyancy to easily float the diver on the surface.

Unfortunately, this same characteristic also becomes a disadvantage at depths in excess of 50 feet, where the pressure of the water will compress the tiny air bubbles considerably. Generally, the deeper the dive, the colder the water; and the less, the insulating value of the wet suit. Also, as the foam neoprene is compressed, its buoyancy is decreased. The wet suit must be stored carefully. Hang it on padded hangers to prevent rupture of the air bubbles and the formation of permanent creases which will cause loss of insulation.

Wet Suit

INFLATABLE DIVING SUIT

A unique suit design is rapidly becoming standard equipment for many commercial divers and an increasing number of sport divers. The inflatable diving suit is made from ¼″ closed-cell neoprene with waterproof neck, wrist and face seals. Boots and hood are integral components of this flexible design. Entry is gained through a large opening which is sealed by a special water and pressure tight zipper.

The suit is connected to the low pressure port of the scuba regulator by quick disconnect hose and by depressing a button on the suit's air intake valve, air flows into the suit to eliminate suit squeeze and stabilize buoyancy. Depressing the exhaust control button vents the air from the suit. The inflatable diving suit thereby provides the diver with a built-in buoyancy control. Used with a special nylon "fur" underwear, the inflatable diving suit is perhaps the best thermal protection that underwater technology has thus far produced for the diver.

WEIGHT BELT

In addition to the diver's natural buoyancy and that added by the exposure suit, an empty scuba cylinder will add to the diver's positive buoyancy.

The compressed air in a fully charged tank adds approximately 5 pounds to its weight. As this air is exhausted, the equipment becomes increasingly more buoyant and will actually float when empty. Since the sport diver, ideally, swims in a state of near weightlessness, it is necessary to neutralize this tendency to float through the proper use of weights.

The ideal weight belt is a strong 2 inch wide nylon belt fitted with a rugged, corrosion-resistant buckle which can be quickly-released with one hand. Slotted lead weights of varying sizes can be easily slipped on to the belt to adjust the diver's bouyancy to near weightlessness.

To determine the amount of weight necessary to achieve neutral bouyancy, put on all your equipment and enter the water wearing about 10 pounds of weight. Descend a few feet, preferably down an anchor line. Remove or add one weight at a time until you achieve a state of balance where, on inhaling you will tend to rise and descend while exhaling. Remember, the "wet suit" will compress on descent and on dives of 50 feet or more, the diver will require less weight. Due to the greater density of sea water, you will

Inflatable Diving Suit

require more weight than for a similar dive in fresh water. Lastly, the weight belt is the last piece of equipment secured to the diver so that in an emergency, it can be ditched quickly.

ACUTE CHECKOUT-ITIS

Acute Checkout-itis is a common, one-time malady (like the mumps and measels) that invariably strikes just before the student diver's first open water dive.

Although there is no predictable pattern to the development of the symptoms of acute checkout-itis, they are quite distinctive and readily recognized.

The student diver may suffer:

1) loss of appetite   5) sweating palms
2) loss of memory   6) dry throat
3) loss of breakfast   7) slack jaw
4) excessive perspiration   8) vacant stare

The symptoms described above may be accompanied by noticeable knee trembling, although this is not considered a reliable sign.

Acute checkout-itis is considered quite common and apparently strikes all student divers. In all probability the scuba instructor has suffered this strange disease himself and will be inclined to be sympathetic.

TREATMENT

Little is known of the exact mechanisms of acute checkout-itis, but it is universally agreed that no treatment is required since all symptoms disappear within five minutes of the start of the dive.

QUESTIONS ON CHAPTER 10

1. When a decompression dive is being planned, what factors must be considered?
2. If at the surface your breathing rate is two (2) cubic feet per minute (c.f.m.), what would it be at a depth of 168 feet (sea water)? How long would a 72 cubic foot tank last at the new rate?
3. A scuba tank rated 72 cubic feet at 2475 p.s.i. is partially charged to 1550 p.s.i. How long would it last at a depth of 96 feet (sea water), based on a surface breathing rate of 0.75 cubic feet per minute?
4. A number of serious effects may result from a diver's exposure to cold water. What are some of these effects?
5. Although trimmed for neutral buoyancy at a depth of 50 feet, on descent to 60 feet a diver, in wet suit and scuba gear, finds himself becoming increasingly negative. Explain.
6. Describe the principle of the wet suit.
7. Describe the principle of the dry suit.
8. Step-by-step, plan a wreck dive in detail. Calculate decompression for a depth of 100 feet (sea water) and a bottom time of 60 minutes.
9. Explain the relationship between decompression and recompression in the treatment of decompression sickness.
10. Two dives are planned to salvage two (2) bronze portholes from an ocean shipwreck at a depth of 120 feet. Your surface breathing rate is one (1) c.f.m. Approximately 10 minutes are required to remove each porthole. Providing for decompression stops (if any) can each dive be made with a 72 cubic foot tank within a three hour period?

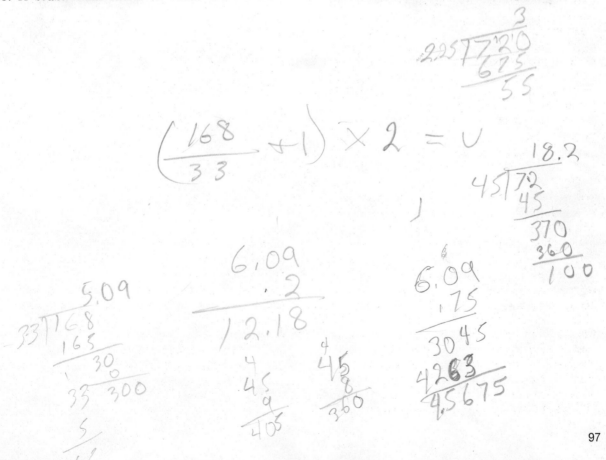

Chapter 11   DIVING SKILLS

Presuming the student-diver has successfully completed the swimming prerequisites outlined in the first chapter, he will find the fundamental skills of sport diving are easily mastered.

Determination and practice provide the key to the prompt development of these skills. While the fledgling diver may tend to be a little uncertain at times in his first attempts at underwater breathing, he will discover that as his proficiency increases with practice his confidence grows correspondingly.

FACE MASK

The mask has been called the diver's "magic looking glass" for it is only through the mask that the secrets of the underwater world reveal themselves. As previously noted, the basic function of the mask is to provide an air space between the diver's eyes and the water. The selection of mask most suitable to a particular diver is pretty much a question of individual preference. However, certain qualities are common to all good masks. Above all, it should be sufficiently flexible to fit the contours of the face comfortably and must provide a positive seal to prevent water leaks. The lens should be made of shatterproof glass and secured to the mask body by a removeable metal band. The split head strap should be easily adjustable through firmly secured mask strap clamps.

FITTING THE MASK

To determine if the mask seals over your eyes and nose comfortably, put the mask in place without the head strap, inhale slightly through the nose and remove your hands. The mask should cling to the face until the breath is released. A good seal is thus insured.

LENS FOGGING

During a dive, the inside of the mask lens may "fog" with condensation due to the difference in the temperatures of the diver's skin and the colder surrounding water. There are several procedures for minimizing the "fogging" effect. The inside of a mask lens may be cleaned with a commercial anti-fogging solution (e.g. Dacor De-Fog) and rinsed. Still another effective and readily available anti-fogging substance is saliva. Some divers solve the "fogging" problem by carrying a small amount of water in the bottom of the mask. If the lens begins to fog, the diver faces down and rolls his head slowly, allowing the trapped water to rinse away the condensation.

MASK CLEARING (VERTICAL)

The "mask clearing" skill is one of the easiest to learn, and it is so vitally important to his safety in the water that the student-diver must practice this skill until it becomes instinctive. When the trained diver's mask is accidentally knocked loose, he simply seals the high side of the mask, puffs air through his nose and expels the water. Knowledge of the corrective procedures reduces mask flooding from a dangerous situation to an occasional irritant for the trained diver.

The untrained diver at this moment is close to panic, however, and may perish as a result of his lack of training. Try a simple test right now! Sitting upright, exert a gentle pressure against your forehead with your fingertips. While keeping your eyes open and your lips sealed, exhale short puffs of air through the nostrils. Now, roll your head back slightly until you can see the ceiling and exhale again. You have now

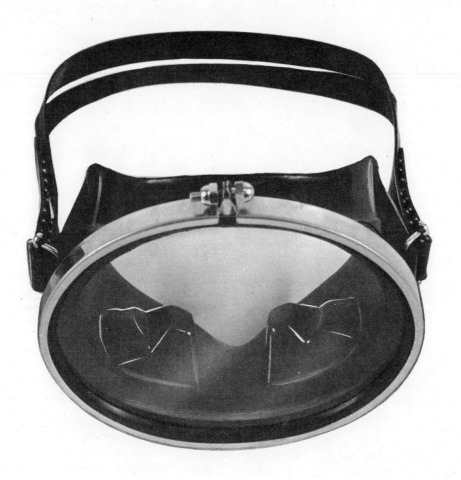

Mask

learned the secret of mask clearing and only require shallow-water practice.

Let's review those steps. Presuming the mask is properly seated on your face, exerting gentle pressure against the upper rim of the mask will trap the air exhaled through the nostrils. As the air rises to the top of the mask with each puff, the water level inside the mask will drop. Since the air is displacing the water, the diver keeps his eyes open to see precisely how much air is required to clear all the water from the mask. Usually a small volume of water will remain trapped at the lower edge of the lens. The diver rolls his head back to drain the remaining water back toward the skirt where it can be purged from the mask. To prevent water from rolling back into the nose, exhale air through the nostrils before rolling the head back.

Vertical Clearing

Horizontal Clearing

MASK CLEARING (HORIZONTAL)

Having observed that exhaled air always goes up, it is evident that the mask may be cleared from virtually any position provided the diver seals the mask in such a manner to trap the exhaled air. The student-diver should practice clearing the mask in all conceiveable positions and sealing the mask alternately with either hand. While in a horizontal position, the diver rolls on his side so that either of the shoulders is pointed toward the surface. The upper rim of the mask *(the side nearest the surface)* is sealed by gentle pressure exerted with the palm. Again, short puffs of air are exhaled through the nose with the eyes held open until the water level has receded to its lowest point. Again, it will be necessary to roll the head so the water in the low spot of the mask drains to the skirt from where it can be cleared.

"NO HANDS" CLEARING

In the event of mask flooding while the diver's hands are full, the mask can be cleared of water without the use of hands. Tilt your head back until the mask is pointed directly at the surface and exhale through your nose. The air will build up and force the water out. To determine how much water remains in the mask between puffs, roll your head forward to drain the remaining water into the bottom of the mask.

SNORKEL

The snorkel may be the diver's most foolproof piece of equipment. Containing no moving parts,

it is simply a breathing tube that enables the diver to swim effortlessly on the surface. It allows the diver to breathe comfortably without requiring that he lift his head from the water to breathe, an effort which may rob the surface swimmer of up to 30% of his energy. The diver thus equipped is enabled to swim long distances without becoming tired. It is also useful to the scuba diver, for it allows him to conserve his cylinder air while he swims out on the surface to his diving site. It is his primary piece of life-saving equipment when he surfaces after a dive, a long distance from his base of operations. Although there are many types of snorkels commercially available, they differ little in design or construction. The most popular snorkel is the J-shaped open tube.

WEARING THE SNORKEL

While the exact design selected is a matter of individual preference, the diver should select one which has a comfortable mouthpiece and proper fit. It is normally worn between the mask strap and the head. While in a normal face-down position, it should form a right angle with the water. Unlike some early types of snorkels equipped with ping pong balls and other one-way valves, which theoretically prevented water from

No Hands Clearing

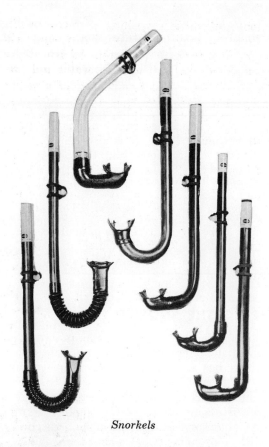

Snorkels

"J" fills with water upon descent, and must be blown clear when the diver surfaces. The diver is thereby compelled to retain sufficient air in his lungs to blow the breathing tube clear before he can resume breathing. The student-diver must keep his lips sealed tightly around the mouthpiece to prevent water from leaking into the mouth. Upon surfacing, the diver exhales sharply into the mouthpiece while gripping the snorkel firmly with his mouth. As a rule, the snorkel will be cleared with the diver's first exhalation. However, the diver should retain a little air in his lungs, and if, upon inhaling cautiously, some water is still present, he can exhale again and resume normal breathing.

DISPLACEMENT CLEARING

A more refined and energy-saving method of snorkel clearing is to expel the water in the snorkel while submerged!

As the diver ascends, his face is tilted up toward the surface, and his snorkel naturally forms an angle approximately 45° to the surface. As the diver gently exhales into the snorkel, the water is displaced through the open end.

Clearing begins when the diver is within 2 feet of the surface. When the surface is broken, the diver rolls into the normal snorkeling position and resumes breathing.

entering the tube, *(which, incidentally, always leaked and are considered dangerous)* the open

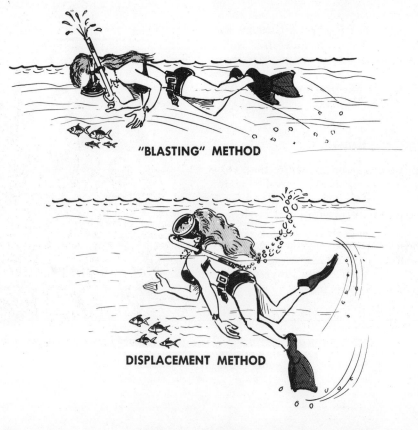

"BLASTING" METHOD

DISPLACEMENT METHOD

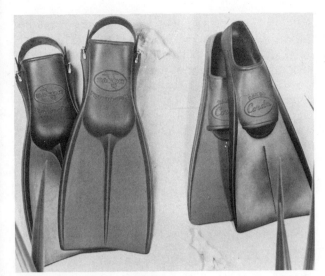

Fins (Adjustable and Full Foot)

THE FINS

The diver's fins are simply extensions of his feet. The sole purpose of the fin is to increase the foot's effective propelling surface enabling the diver to move more efficiently and with greater thrust through the water. All arm strokes are completely ineffective under water and since he is usually using his hands to hold a camera or a spear gun, for example, the diver is to a great degree dependent upon the fins.

There are a multitude of fins available on the commercial market. To aid in his selection of the proper fins, the student-diver may find the review of each of the basic fins helpful in determining the most suitable. Regardless of which fin he selects, the most important consideration is fit. When properly sized, the fin should fit snugly and comfortably on the diver's foot. If the fin is too tight, it will cause foot cramps. Conversely, if it is too loose, it may chafe and blister the foot. Some divers prefer a larger fin and compensate for the loose fit by wearing wet suit boots inside the fin. Fin size generally corresponds to the normal shoe size and a good fit can be thus insured. Generally speaking, there are two basic categories of fins.

Because of its tremendous thrust, the adjustable, power fin is rapidly becoming the favorite of the experienced diver.

Full Foot Pocket

Most neophyte divers select this type fin because the blade is only moderately stiff and provides good thrust and power without tiring the diver. The foot pocket fully covers the foot providing protection against coral, rocks and other sharp objects. These fins are usually available in both floating and non-floating rubbers. The floating fin has the desirable characteristic of being easy to retrieve if lost. Extremely flexible fins should be avoided since they provide little thrust for the energy expended.

Open Heel Fin

The open heel fin has the distinctive advantage of being adjustable to many foot sizes because of its heel strap. Due to its large rigid blade and heavy rails, this type fin may put excessive strain on the leg muscles of the student-diver, and leg cramps may occur. Because of its tremendous thrust, the open-heel, power fin is rapidly becoming the favorite of the experienced diver.

Wearing the Fins

When putting on the fins, wet the feet as well as the fins. Grasp the side rails firmly and work the foot well down into the foot pocket before pulling the heel strap up over the heel. Use both thumbs when pulling on the heel to avoid tearing the strap or heel pocket. If it is necessary to walk in the fins, shuffling backwards will minimize the possibility of bending the blade under and tripping. The most effective method of employing the large propelling area of the fin is the flutter kick.

FLUTTER KICK

In order to exact maximum thrust from the fins, the diver's toes should be extended as much as possible, drawing an imaginary straight line from the hip socket to the fin tip. If the foot is held in the natural walking position while swimming, the efficiency of the fin is reduced substantially. The legs should move like pendulums, pivoting at the hip with a minimum of knee bending. Diving is a lazy man's sport and the diver's primary kick should be correspondingly relaxed. The kicks should be approximately 24" wide and the diver should swim in a slightly head up, back-arched attitude through the water.

Trudgeon Kick

TRUDGEON KICK

When performing the trudgeon kick the diver swims on his side. The legs are held stiff and the toes are extended as in the flutter kick. The legs sweep from side to side, alternately crossing over one another in long, powerful kicks. The trudgeon provides great power and may be particularly useful when towing an object or a tired swimmer back to the base of operations.

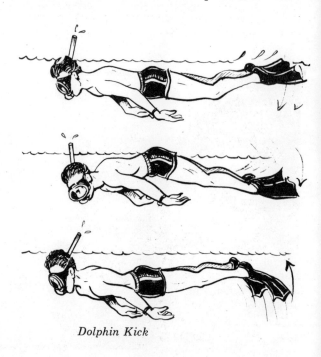

Dolphin Kick

THE DOLPHIN KICK

The dolphin is fundamentally a fun-type kick that emulates the movement of a porpoise. In the dolphin kick, the entire body undulates rhythmically moving the diver rapidly through the water. The diver begins this movement in the prone position. The shoulders are rolled forward smoothly while the feet, held close together, are thrust upward. The back is then

Surface Dive (head first)

arched and the fins thrust downward. The movements should be overexaggerated initially and then refined to smooth, liquid movements.

DIRECTIONAL CONTROL

With a little practice, the student-diver will discover that all movements underwater can be made fluid and smooth by simply using the body to control the direction of movement. When the diver wishes to go deeper, he need only bend at the waist. To ascend, the head is rolled back and the back arched. Smooth turns are made easily by rolling to one side or the other, arching the back and rolling the head back in the desired direction. The flutter kick will provide the necessary power to execute these movements properly.

ENTERING THE WATER

The manner in which a diver enters the water is generally dictated by the situation. When entering the water from a boat with low freeboard, the most common form of entry is the roll-in. The diver sits on the boat's rail, holding his mask and simply rolls backward into the water. In executing any type of entry, the diver must always carefully check the water below him. When entering water with limited visibility, he should ease himself slowly over the side of the boat maintaining a hand hold on the rail. This will prevent any injury resulting from dropping on a submerged obstacle. When entering the water from a high decked vessel, the diver may simply enter the water from the standing position, again holding the mask securely to his face. This should only be attempted where water visibility is sufficiently adequate to insure that the diver will not fall upon submerged objects. The most effective entry is the one most comfortable under the circumstances.

SURFACE DIVES
Head First

Swimming slowly across the surface, the diver bends sharply at the waist while raising his legs upward, out of the water. When executed properly, the legs are perpendicular to the surface of the water, the knees are stiff and the toes are pointed. The weight of his legs out of the water will drive the diver downward effortlessly.

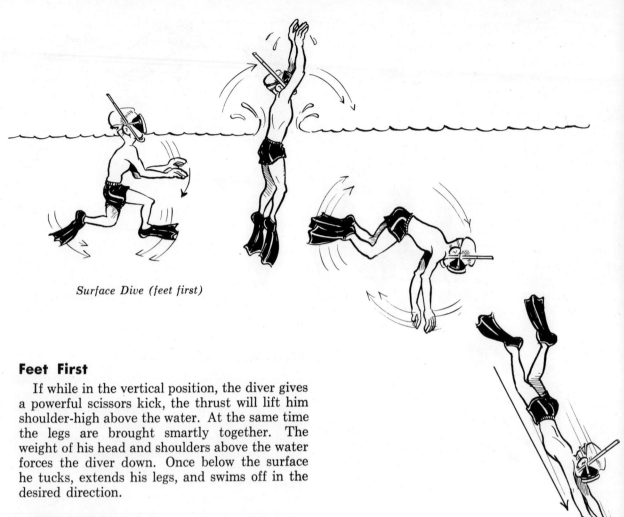

Surface Dive (feet first)

Feet First

If while in the vertical position, the diver gives a powerful scissors kick, the thrust will lift him shoulder-high above the water. At the same time the legs are brought smartly together. The weight of his head and shoulders above the water forces the diver down. Once below the surface he tucks, extends his legs, and swims off in the desired direction.

SCUBA SKILLS

Once a student-diver has recovered from the initial surprise of being able to breathe underwater, he will discover that he tends to breathe more frequently and fill his lungs more than necessary. With practice, he will learn to regulate his breathing and extend his useful time underwater.

Mouthpiece Clearing

As already explained, all two-hose regulators are equipped with non-return valves which prevent water from entering the regulator body and hoses. In the event the mouthpiece is momentarily lost and fills with water, the diver need only replace it and exhale sharply. Any water that may be collected there will be blown into the exhaust hose and out of the regulator. If the hoses should become flooded due to a defective non-return valve, the diver need only raise the mouthpiece above the regulator to start a free flow of air. Once the free flow has started, the

diver replaces the mouthpiece, exhales, and resumes breathing.

"Milking"

Under extraordinary circumstances, the low pressure reduction area of the regulator could be flooded with water, balancing the low pressure diaphragm on both sides with water pressure and preventing an air flow. The diver can easily restore a free flow of air by "milking" the inhalation hose. This is accomplished by reaching back over the right shoulder and squeezing the water toward the mouthpiece by rapidly "milking" the inhalation hose. The milking restores a relative vacuum under the diaphragm and a free flow is started. At this point the mouthpiece should be replaced and the left shoulder dropped so that the water will drain into the exhaust hose. Now, while squeezing off the inhalation hose at the mouthpiece, the diver exhales sharply, clearing the mouthpiece and the exhaust hose of accumulated water.

Single Hose Regulator

Since the second stage diaphragm is housed together with the mouthpiece, there can be no pressure differential between the two and consequently no free flow. However, most single hose regulators are equipped with a purge button which, when pressed, forces the diaphragm inward manually and a free flow thus results. If a single hose regulator has no purge button and the diver finds himself without sufficient lung air to blow the mouthpiece clear, he can easily drink the water in the flooded mouthpiece and restore normal breathing. Due to the size of most single hose regulator mouthpieces, general-

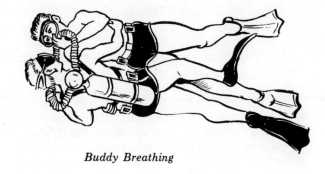

Buddy Breathing

ly less than two ounces of water can be trapped there.

Buddy Breathing

Despite the fact that malfunctions are unheard of with today's high performance scuba equipment, it is imperative to his ultimate safety that the student diver become skilled in the buddy

Buddy Breathing on Ascent

breathing procedure. Two divers can breathe from one operating unit without the slightest wanting for air.

When using a two-hose regulator, the diver wearing the operating scuba swims with his left side down. The diver-buddies swim facing each other maintaining a hand hold on one another's backpack harnesses. The mouthpiece is shuttled back and forth with each buddy taking a breath or two and passing the mouthpiece back. On ascent, the diver awaiting the mouthpiece must exhale to prevent air embolism. Since the mouthpiece will fill with water as it is passed from diver to diver, each diver begins the breathing cycle by first clearing the mouthpiece. This skill should be practiced until the procedure becomes completely routine.

BUDDY BREATHING ON ASCENT

Should the need for buddy breathing occur where the divers are compelled to swim horizontally before they can ascend, (inside a cave or wreck, for example) it would seem logical for one buddy to breath hold while the other took his breaths. On ascent, obviously, breath holding would be a fatal mistake. An excellent, confidence-building exercise is illustrated. With a safety diver overhead, the buddy-breathing divers swim several laps of the pool ending at a buoyed line which is firmly anchored on the bottom. Still sharing air, they ascend *slowly* to the surface. Each controls his ascent with a grip on the buoyed line and exhales continuously *between breaths*, as in an emergency swimming ascent.

DITCH AND RECOVERY

Of all the confidence building maneuvers practiced, the "ditch and recovery" procedure surpasses all other skills in developing the student-diver's confidence.

He learns that no matter how hopelessly his equipment may be fouled, he need only unbuckle and slide free of it while retaining the mouthpiece and continuing to breathe. He is then free to disentangle and replace the equipment.

With practice, the student-diver develops confidence in his own abilities as well as in the reliability and versatility of his equipment. It is this confidence that will enable him to quickly analyze and avoid potentially dangerous situations underwater. This skill must only be practiced in the presence of a qualified scuba instructor.

Ditch and Recovery

DITCHING

While seated or kneeling on the pool bottom, the student-diver first removes his fins and snorkel and places them to one side. The weight belt is then unbuckled and positioned across the lap or the raised knee. The quick-release buckle on the waist strap is now released. The diver reaches back and swings the tank over his head, standing it in front of him with the regulator at eye level. The cylinder valve is turned off and the mouthpiece removed. The tank is then laid carefully on its side and the weight belt placed over the tank bottom. The mask is removed and placed next to the regulator. The diver exhales and begins a free ascent to the surface. The importance of continuous exhalation on ascent cannot be overemphasized.

Bail Out

RECOVERING

The student-diver surface-dives to the bottom and sits or kneels beside his equipment. First, the weight belt is placed across the lap or knee and the tank stood on end. The cylinder air valve is turned on, the mouthpiece recovered and cleared, and breathing restored. Next, the mask is reseated over the face and cleared. When properly positioned, the backside of the regulator should be facing the diver. The tank is grasped at its sides and swung over the head.

The shoulder harness will fall into proper position as the tank swings overhead. When the tank is in place, the waist strap quick-release is secured. If using a two-hose regulator, the diver now reaches back and traces the hoses from the regulator to the mouthpiece to insure against twists which might pinch off the air supply. If a twist is found, the mouthpiece is removed, the hose untwisted, and the mouthpiece reinserted and cleared. The weight belt is refastened around the waist, the fins and snorkel replaced and the diver makes a normal ascent.

BAIL OUT

This great confidence-builder is essentially the recovery phase of a "ditch and recovery". The only real difference is that the exercise begins with the diver standing on the pool deck with all the equipment already in his hands. The object is to keep buoyancy and equipment under control while completing the recovery. A systematic approach to this exercise goes a long way to keeping it simple. Study the illustration! Note that the diver has slipped the mask over his wrist. The snorkel is tucked into a fin pocket. And the weight belt is buckled and rests over the shoulder. In this manner, it is not likely that any equipment will be lost when he enters the water.

QUESTIONS ON CHAPTER 11

1. Although the face mask provides clear vision underwater, it also tends to distort vision. Why?
2. What are the four steps in "clearing" a mask underwater?
3. Why should a sport diver *ALWAYS* carry a snorkel?
4. List three (3) methods for "equalizing" your ears.
5. On a breath-holding dive to 20 feet a skin diver finds his mask pressed uncomfortably tight against his face. What has caused this and how can it be remedied?
6. Describe four (4) methods for "clearing" flooded regulator mouthpieces and hoses.
7. Explain the "milking" procedure. What circumstances would require this method?
8. Describe the "buddy breathing" procedure.
9. Of what practical advantage is training in the ditch and recovery procedure.
10. Detail your procedure should your scuba suddenly become inoperative at a depth of 100 feet.

APPENDICES

APPENDIX A

REFERENCES FOR ADDITIONAL STUDY

U.S. Navy Diving Manual
Superintendent of Documents
U.S. Government Printing Office

Underwater Physiology
(Symposium Proceedings)
Williams & Wilkins Company

The Physiology and Medicine
of Diving and Compressed Air Work
Edited by: *P. B. Bennett and D. H. Elliott*
Williams & Wilkins Company

Medical Aspects of Sport Diving
by *Christopher Dueker*
A. S. Barnes and Company

Underwater Medicine
by *Stanley Miles*
J. B. Lippincott

Man Under The Sea
by *James Dugan*
Harper & Brothers

Undersea Explorer
by *James Dugan*
Harper & Brothers

Human Performance and Scuba Diving
(Symposium Proceedings)
The Athletic Institute

Research Diver's Manual
by *Lee Somers*
University of Michigan

The Sea Around Us
by *Rachel Carlson*
Oxford University Press

Seven Miles Down
by *Jacques Piccard and Robert Dietz*
G. P. Putnam and Sons

Our World Underwater
by *William Stephens*
Lantern Press

Survival in Cold Water
by *W. R. Keatinge*
Blackwell Scientific Publications

Safe Cave Diving
by *Tom Mount*
National Association for Cave Diving

Life Saving and Water Safety
by *Charles Silvia*
Association Press

Marine Salvage Operations
by *Edward M. Brady*
Cornell Maritime Press

Archaeology Under Water
by *George F. Bass*
Frederick A. Praeger Co.

History Under The Sea
by *Mendel Peterson*
Smithsonian Institution

Deep Diving and Submarine Operations
by *Sir Robert Henry Davis*
St. Catherine Press

Underwater Guide to Marine Life
by *Carlton Ray and Elgin Ciampi*
A. S. Barnes and Company, Inc.

Dangerous Marine Animals
by *Bruce W. Halstead*
Cornell Maritime Press

Divers And Cameras
by *Joe Strykowski*
Dacor

Underwater Work
by *John E. Cayford*
Cornell Maritime Press

The Treasure Diver's Guide
by *John S. Potter, Jr.*
Doubleday and Co., Inc.

The Treasure Divers of Vigo Bay
by *John S. Potter, Jr.*
Doubleday and Co., Inc.

Standards for Cardio Pulmonary
Resuscitation (CPR) and Emergency
Cardiac Care (ECC)
American Heart Association

Camera Below
by *Hank Frey and Paul Tzimoulis*
Association Press

UNDERWATER MAGAZINES

Skin Diver
5900 Hollywood Boulevard
Los Angeles, California 90028

Dive Magazine
P. O. Box 7765
Long Beach, California 90807

Aquarius
1757 Long Beach Boulevard
Long Beach, California 90813

APPENDIX B

U.S. NAVY STANDARD AIR DECOMPRESSION TABLE

All dives beyond the limits of the No-Decompression Table require decompression stops (specified depths at which a diver must remain for a specified length of time to eliminate inert gas from his body). These dives are listed in the U.S. NAVY STANDARD AIR DECOMPRESSION TABLE. These tables represent the best overall information available, but as depth and time increases, they tend to be less accurate and require careful application. Lacking the presence of a trained Diving Medical Officer or someone otherwise qualified, the tables must be rigidly followed to ensure maximum diving safety. Variations in decompression procedures are permissible only with the guidance of a qualified diving medical officer in emergency situations.

If the bottom time of a dive is less than the first bottom time listed for its depth, decompression is not required. The diver may ascend directly to the surface at a rate of 60 feet per minute. The repetitive group designation for no-decompression dives is given in the No-Decompression Table.

SELECTION OF DECOMPRESSION SCHEDULE

A decompression schedule is a specific decompression procedure for a given combination of depth and bottom time as listed in a decompression table; it is normally indicated as feet/minutes. The decompression schedules of all the tables are given in 10 or 20-foot depth increments and, usually, 10-minute bottom time increments. Depth and bottom time combinations from actual dives, however, rarely exactly match one of the decompression schedules listed in the table being used. As assurance that the selected decompression schedule is always conservative—(A) always select the schedule depth (the maximum depth attained during the dive, measured in feet of seawater (fsw) to be equal to or the next depth greater than the actual depth to which the dive was conducted, and (B) always select the schedule bottom time to be equal to or the next longer bottom time than the actual bottom time of the dive.

If the Standard Air Decompression Table, for example, was being used to select the correct schedule for a dive to 97 feet for 31 minutes, decompression would be carried out in accordance with the 100/40 schedule.

NEVER ATTEMPT TO INTERPOLATE BETWEEN DECOMPRESSION SCHEDULES

If the diver was exceptionally cold during the dive, or if his work load was relatively strenuous, the next longer decompression schedule than the one he would normally follow should be selected. For example, the normal schedule for a dive to 90 feet for 34 minutes would be the 90/40 schedule. If the diver were exceptionally cold or fatigued, he should decompress according to the 90/50 schedule.

Example—
Problem—Diver Bowman has just completed a salvage dive to a depth of 143 feet for 37 minutes. He was not exceptionally cold or fatigued during the dive. What is his decompression schedule and his repetitive group designation at the end of the decompression?

Solution—Select the equal or next deeper and the equal or next longer decompression schedule. This would be the 150/40 schedule.

Courtesy of United States Navy

115

ACTION	TIME (min:sec)	TOTAL ELAPSED ASCENT TIME (min:sec)
Ascend to 30 feet at 60 fpm	1:53	1:53
Remain at 30 feet	5:00	6:53
Ascend to 20 feet	0.10	7:03
Remain at 20 feet	19:00	26.03
Ascend to 10 feet	0.10	26:13
Remain at 10 feet	33:00	59:13
Ascend to surface	0:10	59:23

Repetitive Group Designation   "N"

Rules During Ascent After the correct decompression schedule has been selected, it is imperative that it be exactly followed. Without exception, decompression must be completed according to the selected schedule unless the directions to alter the schedule are given by a diving medical officer.

Ascend at a rate of 60 feet per minute. Any variation in the rate of ascent must be corrected. The diver's chest should be located as close as possible to the stop depth. A pneumofathometer is the most practical instrument for ensuring proper measurement.

The decompression stop times, as specified in each decompression schedule, begin as soon as the diver reaches the stop depth. Upon completion of the specified stop time, the diver ascends to the next stop, or to the surface, at the proper ascent rate. DO NOT INCLUDE ASCENT TIME AS PART OF STOP TIME.

VARIATIONS IN RATE OF ASCENT

Since conditions sometimes prevent these ascent rates from being maintained, a general set of instructions has been established to compensate for any variations in rate of ascent. These instructions, along with examples of their application are:

Example No. 1—
Condition—Rate of ascent less than 60 fpm, delay occurs greater than 50 fsw.

Procedure—Increase BOTTOM TIME by the difference between the actual ascent time and the time if 60 fpm were used.

A dive was conducted to 120 feet with a bottom time of 60 minutes. According to the 120/60 decompression schedule of the Standard Air Decompression Table, the first decompression stop is at 30 feet. During the ascent the diver was delayed at 100 feet and it actually took 5 minutes for him to reach his 30 foot decompression stop. If an ascent rate of 60 fpm were used, it would have taken him 1 minute 30 seconds to ascend from 120 feet to 30 feet. The difference between the actual and 60 fpm ascent times is 3 minutes 30 seconds. Increase the bottom time of the dive from 60 minutes to 63 minutes 30 seconds and continue decompression according to the schedule which represents this new bottom time . . . the 120/70 schedule. (Note from the Standard Air Decompression Table that this 3 minute 30 second delay increased the diver's total decompression time from 71 minutes to 92 minutes 30 seconds—an increase of 21 minutes 30 seconds).

Example No. 2—
Condition—Rate of ascent less than 60 fpm delay occurs less than 50 fsw.

Procedure—Increase TIME OF FIRST DECOMPRESSION STOP by difference between the actual ascent time and the time if 60 fpm were used.

A dive was conducted to 120 feet with a bottom time of 60 minutes. From the Standard Air Decompression Table the first decompression stop is at 30 fsw. During the ascent, the diver was delayed at 40 feet and it actually took 5 minutes for him to reach his 30-foot stop. As in the preceding example, the correct ascent time should have been 1 minute 30 seconds causing a delay of 3 minutes 30 seconds. Increase the length of the 30 foot decompression stop by 3 minutes 30 seconds. Instead of 2 minutes, the diver must spend 5 minutes 30 seconds at 30 feet. (Note that in this example, the diver's total decompression time is increased by only 7 minutes; the 3 minute 30 second delay in ascent plus the additional 3 minutes 30 seconds he had to spend at 30 feet).

Example No. 3—
Condition—Rate of ascent greater than 60 fpm, no decompression required, bottom time places the diver within 10 minutes of decompression schedule requiring decompression.

Procedure—Stop at 10 feet for the time that it would have taken to ascend at a rate of 60 fpm.

A dive was conducted to 100 feet with a bottom time of 22 minutes. During ascent, the diver momentarily lost control of his buoyancy and increased his ascent rate to 75 fpm. Normally, the 100/25 decompression schedule of the Standard Air Decompression Table would be used, which is a no-decom-

pression schedule. However, the actual bottom time of 22 minutes is within 10 minutes of the 100/30 dive schedule which does require decompression. The diver must stop at 10 feet and remain there for 1 minute and 40 seconds, the time that it would have taken him to ascend at 60 fpm.

Example No. 4—
Condition—Rate of ascent greater than 60 fpm, decompression required.

Procedure—Stop 10 feet below the first decompression stop for the remaining time that it would have taken if a rate of 60 fpm were used.

A diver ascending from a 120/50 scheduled dive takes only 30 seconds to reach his 20-foot decompression stop. At a rate of 60 fpm his ascent time should have been 1 minute 40 seconds. He must return to 30 feet and remain there for the difference between 1 minute 40 seconds and 30 seconds, or 1 minute 10 seconds.

The rate of ascent between stops is not critical, and variations from the specified rate require no compensation.

Note:
When using the dive tables, be particularly careful to enter and move across the table tabulations on a straight line. To avoid inadvertently slipping off a line and selecting the wrong (and possibly dangerous) data, use a straight-edge or ruler to stay aligned in a given column.

Courtesy of United States Navy

U. S. NAVY STANDARD AIR DECOMPRESSION TABLE

Depth (feet)	Bottom time (min)	Time first stop (min:sec)	Decompression stops (feet)					Total ascent (min:sec)	Repetitive group
			50	40	30	20	10		
40	200						0	0:40	*
	210	0:30					2	2:40	N
	230	0:30					7	7:40	N
	250	0:30					11	11:40	O
	270	0:30					15	15:40	O
	300	0:30					19	19:40	Z
50	100						0	0:50	*
	110	0:40					3	3:50	L
	120	0:40					5	5:50	M
	140	0:40					10	10:50	M
	160	0:40					21	21:50	N
	180	0:40					29	29:50	O
	200	0:40					35	35:50	O
	220	0:40					40	40:50	Z
	240	0:40					47	47:50	Z
60	60						0	1:00	*
	70	0:50					2	3:00	K
	80	0:50					7	8:00	L
	100	0:50					14	15:00	M
	120	0:50					26	27:00	N
	140	0:50					39	40:00	O
	160	0:50					48	49:00	Z
	180	0:50					56	57:00	Z
	200	0:40				1	69	71:00	Z
70	50						0	1:10	*
	60	1:00					8	9:10	K
	70	1:00					14	15:10	L
	80	1:00					18	19:10	M
	90	1:00					23	24:10	N
	100	1:00					33	34:10	N
	110	0:50				2	41	44:10	O
	120	0:50				4	47	52:10	O
	130	0:50				6	52	59:10	O
	140	0:50				8	56	65:10	Z
	150	0:50				9	61	71:10	Z
	160	0:50				13	72	86:10	Z
	170	0:50				19	79	99:10	Z

* See No Decompression Table for repetitive groups

Courtesy of United States Navy

U.S. NAVY STANDARD AIR DECOMPRESSION TABLE

Depth (feet)	Bottom time (min)	Time first stop (min:sec)	Decompression stops (feet) 50	40	30	20	10	Total ascent (min:sec)	Repetitive group
80	40						0	1:20	*
	50	1:10					10	11:20	K
	60	1:10					17	18:20	L
	70	1:10					23	24:20	M
	80	1:00				2	31	34:20	N
	90	1:00				7	39	47:20	N
	100	1:00				11	46	58:20	O
	110	1:00				13	53	67:20	O
	120	1:00				17	56	74:20	Z
	130	1:00				19	63	83:20	Z
	140	1:00				26	69	96:20	Z
	150	1:00				32	77	110:20	Z
90	30						0	1:30	*
	40	1:20					7	8:30	J
	50	1:20					18	19:30	L
	60	1:20					25	26:30	M
	70	1:10				7	30	38:30	N
	80	1:10				13	40	54:30	N
	90	1:10				18	48	67:30	O
	100	1:10				21	54	76:30	Z
	110	1:10				24	61	86:30	Z
	120	1:10				32	68	101:30	Z
	130	1:00			5	36	74	116:30	Z
100	25						0	1:40	*
	30	1:30					3	4:40	I
	40	1:30					15	16:40	K
	50	1:20				2	24	27:40	L
	60	1:20				9	28	38:40	N
	70	1:20				17	39	57:40	O
	80	1:20				23	48	72:40	O
	90	1:10			3	23	57	84:40	Z
	100	1:10			7	23	66	97:40	Z
	110	1:10			10	34	72	117:40	Z
	120	1:10			12	41	78	132:40	Z
110	20						0	1:50	*
	25	1:40					3	4:50	H
	30	1:40					7	8:50	J
	40	1:30				2	21	24:50	L
	50	1:30				8	26	35:50	M
	60	1:30				18	36	55:50	N
	70	1:20			1	23	48	73:50	O
	80	1:20			7	23	57	88:50	Z
	90	1:20			12	30	64	107:50	Z
	100	1:20			15	37	72	125:50	Z

See No Decompression Table for repetitive groups

Courtesy of United States Navy

U. S. NAVY STANDARD AIR DECOMPRESSION TABLE

120

Depth (feet)	Bottom time (min)	Time to first stop (min:sec)	Decompression stops (feet) 70	60	50	40	30	20	10	Total ascent (min:sec)	Repetitive group
120	15								0	2:00	*
	20	1:50							2	4:00	H
	25	1:50							6	8:00	I
	30	1:50							14	16:00	J
	40	1:40						5	25	32:00	L
	50	1:40						15	31	48:00	N
	60	1:30					2	22	45	71:00	O
	70	1:30					9	23	55	89:00	O
	80	1:30					15	27	63	107:00	Z
	90	1:30					19	37	74	132:00	Z
	100	1:30					23	45	80	150:00	Z

130

Depth (feet)	Bottom time (min)	Time to first stop (min:sec)	Decompression stops (feet) 70	60	50	40	30	20	10	Total ascent (min:sec)	Repetitive group
130	10								0	2:10	*
	15	2:00							1	3:10	F
	20	2:00							4	6:10	H
	25	2:00							10	12:10	J
	30	1:50					3		18	23:10	M
	40	1:50						10	25	37:10	N
	50	1:40					3	21	37	63:10	O
	60	1:40					9	23	52	86:10	Z
	70	1:40					16	24	61	103:10	Z
	80	1:30				3	19	35	72	131:10	Z
	90	1:30				8	19	45	80	154:10	Z

140

Depth (feet)	Bottom time (min)	Time to first stop (min:sec)	Decompression stops (feet) 90	80	70	60	50	40	30	20	10	Total ascent (min:sec)	Repetitive group
140	10										0	2:20	*
	15	2:10									2	4:20	G
	20	2:10									6	8:20	I
	25	2:00								2	14	18:20	J
	30	2:00								5	21	28:20	K
	40	1:50							2	16	26	46:20	N
	50	1:50							6	24	44	76:20	O
	60	1:50							16	23	56	97:20	Z
	70	1:40						4	19	32	68	125:20	Z
	80	1:40						10	23	41	79	155:20	Z

* See No Decompression Table for repetitive groups

Courtesy of United States Navy

U. S. NAVY STANDARD AIR DECOMPRESSION TABLE

150 / 160

Depth (feet)	Bottom time (min)	Time to first stop (min:sec)	90	80	70	60	50	40	30	20	10	Total ascent (min:sec)	Repetitive group
150	5										0	2:30	C
	10	2:20									1	3:30	E
	15	2:20									3	5:30	G
	20	2:10								2	7	11:30	H
	25	2:10								4	17	23:30	K
	30	2:10								8	24	34:30	L
	40	2:00							5	19	33	59:30	N
	50	2:00							12	23	51	88:30	O
	60	1:50						3	19	26	62	112:30	Z
	70	1:50						11	19	39	75	146:30	Z
	80	1:40					1	17	19	50	84	173:30	Z
160	5										0	2:40	D
	10	2:30									1	3:40	F
	15	2:20								1	4	7:40	H
	20	2:20								3	11	16:40	J
	25	2:20								7	20	29:40	K
	30	2:10							2	11	25	40:40	M
	40	2:10							7	23	39	71:40	N
	50	2:00						2	16	23	55	98:40	Z
	60	2:00						9	19	33	69	132:40	Z

170 / 180 / 190

Depth (feet)	Bottom time (min)	Time to first stop (min:sec)	110	100	90	80	70	60	50	40	30	20	10	Total ascent (min:sec)	Repetitive group
170	5												0	2:50	D
	10	2:40											2	4:50	F
	15	2:30										2	5	9:50	H
	20	2:30										4	15	21:50	J
	25	2:20									2	7	23	34:50	L
	30	2:20									4	13	26	45:50	M
	40	2:10								1	10	23	45	81:50	O
	50	2:10								5	18	23	61	109:50	Z
	60	2:00							2	15	22	37	74	152:50	Z
180	5												0	3:00	D
	10	2:50											3	6:00	F
	15	2:40										3	6	12:00	I
	20	2:30									1	5	17	26:00	K
	25	2:30									3	10	24	40:00	L
	30	2:30									6	17	27	53:00	N
	40	2:20								3	14	23	50	93:00	O
	50	2:10							2	9	19	30	65	128:00	Z
	60	2:10							5	16	19	44	81	168:00	Z
190	5												0	3:10	D
	10	2:50										1	3	7:10	G
	15	2:50										4	7	14:10	I
	20	2:40									2	6	20	31:10	K
	25	2:40									5	11	25	44:10	M
	30	2:30								1	8	19	43	63:10	N
	40	2:30								8	14	23	55	103:10	O

Courtesy of United States Navy

APPENDIX C
REPETITIVE DIVE TABLES AND WORKSHEET

Repetitive Dives During the 12-hour period after an air dive, the quantity of residual nitrogen in a diver's body will gradually reduce to its normal level. If, within this period, the diver is to make a second dive—called a repetitive dive—he must consider his present residual nitrogen level when planning for the dive.

The procedures for conducting a repetitive dive are summarized in Figure 7-1. Upon completing his first dive, the diver will have a Repetitive Group Designation assigned to him by either the Standard Air Table or the No-Decompression Table. This designation relates directly to his residual nitrogen level upon surfacing. As nitrogen passes out of his tissues and blood, his repetitive group designation changes. The Residual Nitrogen Table permits this designation to be determined at any time during the surface interval.

Just prior to beginning the repetitive dive, the residual nitrogen time should be determined using the Residual Nitrogen Table. This time is added to the actual bottom time of the repetitive dive to give the bottom time of the **equivalent single dive**. Decompression from the repetitive dive is conducted using the depth and bottom time of the equivalent single dive to select the appropriate decompression schedule. Equivalent single dives which require the use of exceptional exposure decompression schedules should, whenever possible, be avoided.

To assist in determining the decompression schedule for a repetitive dive, a systematic **repetitive dive worksheet**, shown in Figure 7-2, should **always** be used.

If still another dive is to follow the repetitive dive, the depth and bottom time of the first equivalent single dive should be inserted in part I of the second repetitive dive worksheet.

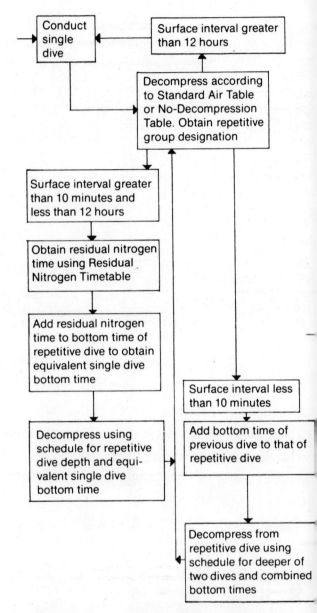

Figure 7-1   Repetitive Dive Flowchart

Courtesy of United States Navy

No-Decompression Limits and Repetitive Group Designation Table for No-Decompression Air Dives

The No-Decompression Table serves two purposes. First it summarizes all the depth and bottom time combinations for which no decompression is required. Secondly, it provides the repetitive group designation for each no-decompression dive. Even though decompression is not required, an amount of nitrogen remains in the diver's tissues after every dive. If he dives again within a 12 hour period, the diver must consider this residual nitrogen when calculating his decompression.

Each depth listed in the No-Decompression Table has a corresponding **no-decompression limit** given in minutes. This limit is the maximum bottom time that a diver may spend at that depth without requiring decompression. The columns to the right of the no-decompression limits column are used to determine the repetitive group designation which must be assigned to a diver subsequent to every dive. To find the repetitive group designation enter the table at the depth equal to or next greater than the actual depth of the dive. Follow that row to the right to the bottom time equal to or next greater than the actual bottom time of the dive. Follow that column upward to the repetitive group designation.

Depths above 35 feet do not have a specific no-decompression limit. They are, however, restricted in that they only provide repetitive group designations for bottom times up to between 5 and 6 hours. These bottom times are considered the limitations of the No-Decompression Table and no field requirement for diving should extend beyond them.

Any dive below 35 feet which has a bottom time greater than the no-decompression limit given in this table is a decompression dive and should be conducted in accordance with the Standard Air Table.

Example—

Problem— In planning a dive, the Master Diver wants to conduct a brief inspection of the work site, located 160 feet below the surface. What is the maximum bottom time which he may use without requiring decompression? What is his repetitive group designation after the dive?

Solution— The no-decompression limit corresponding to the 160 foot depth in the No-Decompression Table is 5 minutes. Therefore, the Master Diver must descend to 160 feet, make his inspection and begin his ascent within 5 minutes without having to undergo decompression.

Following the 160 foot depth row to the 5 minute column, the repetitive group designation at the top of this column is D.

NO-DECOMPRESSION LIMITS AND REPETITIVE GROUP DESIGNATION TABLE FOR NO-DECOMPRESSION AIR DIVES

Depth (feet)	No-decompression limits (min)	A	B	C	D	E	F	G	H	I	J	K	L	M	N	O
10		60	120	210	300											
15		35	70	110	160	225	350									
20		25	50	75	100	135	180	240	325							
25		20	35	55	75	100	125	160	195	245	315					
30		15	30	45	60	75	95	120	145	170	205	250	310			
35	310	5	15	25	40	50	60	80	100	120	140	160	190	220	270	310
40	200	5	15	25	30	40	50	70	80	100	110	130	150	170	200	
50	100		10	15	25	30	40	50	60	70	80	90	100			
60	60		10	15	20	25	30	40	50	55	60					
70	50		5	10	15	20	30	35	40	45	50					
80	40		5	10	15	20	25	30	35	40						
90	30		5	10	12	15	20	25	30							
100	25		5	7	10	15	20	22	25							
110	20			5	10	13	15	20								
120	15			5	10	12	15									
130	10			5	8	10										
140	10			5	7	10										
150	5			5												
160	5				5											
170	5				5											
180	5				5											
190	5				5											

Courtesy of
United States Navy

Residual Nitrogen Timetable for Repetitive Air Dives

The quantity of residual nitrogen in a diver's body immediately after a dive is expressed by the repetitive group designation assigned to him by either the Standard Air Table or the No-Decompression Table. The upper portion of the Residual Nitrogen Table is composed of various intervals between 10 minutes and 12 hours, expressed in minutes: hours (2:21 = 2 hours 21 minutes). Each interval has two limits; a minimum time (top limit) and a maximum time (bottom limit).

Residual nitrogen times, corresponding to the depth of the repetitive dive, are given in the body of the lower portion of the table. To determine the residual nitrogen time for a repetitive dive, locate the diver's repetitive group designation from his previous dive along the diagonal line above the table. Read horizontally to the interval in which the diver's surface interval lies. The time spent on the surface must be between or equal to the limits of the selected interval.

Next, read vertically downwards to the new repetitive group designation. This designation corresponds to the present quantity of residual nitrogen in the diver's body. Continue downward in this same column to the row which represents the depth of the repetitive dive. The time given at the intersection is the residual nitrogen time, in minutes, to be applied to the repetitive dive.

If the surface interval is less than 10 minutes, the residual nitrogen time is the bottom time of the previous dive. All of the residual nitrogen will be passed out of the diver's body after 12 hours, so a dive conducted after a 12 hour surface interval is not a repetitive dive.

There is one exception to this table. In some instances, when the repetitive dive is to the same or greater depth than the previous dive, the residual nitrogen time may be longer than the actual bottom time of the previous dive. In this event, add the actual bottom time of the previous dive to the actual bottom time of the repetitive dive to obtain the equivalent single dive time.

Example—

Problem—A repetitive dive is to be made to 98 fsw for an estimated bottom time of 15 minutes. The previous dive was to a depth of 102 fsw and had a 48 minute bottom time. The diver's surface interval is 6 hours 28 minutes (6:28). What decompression schedule should be used for the repetitive dive?

Solution—Using the repetitive dive worksheet—

REPETITIVE DIVE WORKSHEET

I. PREVIOUS DIVE:
_48_ minutes ✓ Standard Air Table
_102_ feet ☐ No-Decompression Table
_M_ repetitive group designation

II. SURFACE INTERVAL:
_6_ hours _28_ minutes on surface.
Repetitive group from I _M_
New repetitive group from surface
Residual Nitrogen Timetable _B_

III. RESIDUAL NITROGEN TIME:
_98_ feet (depth of repetitive dive)
New repetitive group from II. _B_
Residual nitrogen time from
Residual Nitrogen Timetable _7_

IV. EQUIVALENT SINGLE DIVE TIME:
_7_ minutes, residual nitrogen time from III.
+_15_ minutes, actual bottom time of repetitive dive.
=_22_ minutes, equivalent single dive time.

V. DECOMPRESSION FOR REPETITIVE DIVE:
_22_ minutes, equivalent single dive time from IV.
_98_ feet, depth of repetitive dive

Decompression from (check one):
☐ Standard Air Table ☐ No-Decompression Table
☐ Surface Table Using Oxygen ☐ Surface Table Using Air
✓ No decompression required

Decompression Stops: _____ feet _____ minutes
_____ feet _____ minutes
_____ feet _____ minutes
_____ feet _____ minutes

Schedule used _____ _____ feet _____ minutes
Repetitive group _____

Courtesy of United States Navy

RESIDUAL NITROGEN TIMETABLE FOR REPETITIVE AIR DIVES

*Dives following surface intervals of more than 12 hours are
not repetitive dives. Use actual bottom times in the Standard
Air Decompression Tables to compute decompression for
such dives.

Repetitive group at the beginning of the surface interval

														A	0:10 12:00*
													B	0:10 2:10	2:11 12:00*
												C	0:10 1:39	1:40 2:49	2:50 12:00*
											D	0:10 1:09	1:10 2:38	2:39 5:48	5:49 12:00*
										E	0:10 0:54	0:55 1:57	1:58 3:22	3:23 6:32	6:33 12:00*
									F	0:10 0:45	0:46 1:29	1:30 2:28	2:29 3:57	3:58 7:05	7:06 12:00*
								G	0:10 0:40	0:41 1:15	1:16 1:59	2:00 2:58	2:59 4:25	4:26 7:35	7:36 12:00*
							H	0:10 0:36	0:37 1:06	1:07 1:41	1:42 2:23	2:24 3:20	3:21 4:49	4:50 7:59	8:00 12:00*
						I	0:10 0:33	0:34 0:59	1:00 1:29	1:30 2:02	2:03 2:44	2:45 3:43	3:44 5:12	5:13 8:21	8:22 12:00*
					J	0:10 0:31	0:32 0:54	0:55 1:19	1:20 1:47	1:48 2:20	2:21 3:04	3:05 4:02	4:03 5:40	5:41 8:40	8:41 12:00*
				K	0:10 0:28	0:29 0:49	0:50 1:11	1:12 1:35	1:36 2:03	2:04 2:38	2:39 3:21	3:22 4:19	4:20 5:48	5:49 8:58	8:59 12:00*
			L	0:10 0:26	0:27 0:45	0:46 1:04	1:05 1:25	1:26 1:49	1:50 2:19	2:20 2:53	2:54 3:36	3:37 4:35	4:36 6:02	6:03 9:12	9:13 12:00*
		M	0:10 0:25	0:26 0:42	0:43 0:59	1:00 1:18	1:19 1:39	1:40 2:05	2:06 2:34	2:35 3:08	3:09 3:52	3:53 4:49	4:50 6:18	6:19 9:28	9:29 12:00*
	N	0:10 0:24	0:25 0:39	0:40 0:54	0:55 1:11	1:12 1:30	1:31 1:53	1:54 2:18	2:19 2:47	2:48 3:22	3:23 4:04	4:05 5:03	5:04 6:32	6:33 9:43	9:44 12:00*
O	0:10 0:23	0:24 0:36	0:37 0:51	0:52 1:07	1:08 1:24	1:25 1:43	1:44 2:04	2:05 2:29	2:30 2:59	3:00 3:33	3:34 4:17	4:18 5:16	5:17 6:44	6:45 9:54	9:55 12:00*
0:10 0:22	0:23 0:34	0:35 0:48	0:49 1:02	1:03 1:18	1:19 1:36	1:37 1:55	1:56 2:17	2:18 2:42	2:43 3:10	3:11 3:45	3:46 4:29	4:30 5:27	5:28 6:56	6:57 10:05	10:06 12:00*

NEW → GROUP DESIGNATION	Z	O	N	M	L	K	J	I	H	G	F	E	D	C	B	A

REPETITIVE DIVE DEPTH																
40	257	241	213	187	161	138	116	101	87	73	61	49	37	25	17	7
50	169	160	142	124	111	99	87	76	66	56	47	38	29	21	13	6
60	122	117	107	97	88	79	70	61	52	44	36	30	24	17	11	5
70	100	96	87	80	72	64	57	50	43	37	31	26	20	15	9	4
80	84	80	73	68	61	54	48	43	38	32	28	23	18	13	8	4
90	73	70	64	58	53	47	43	38	33	29	24	20	16	11	7	3
100	64	62	57	52	48	43	38	34	30	26	22	18	14	10	7	3
110	57	55	51	47	42	38	34	31	27	24	20	16	13	10	6	3
120	52	50	46	43	39	35	32	28	25	21	18	15	12	9	6	3
130	46	44	40	38	35	31	28	25	22	19	16	13	11	8	6	3
140	42	40	38	35	32	29	26	23	20	18	15	12	10	7	5	2
150	40	38	35	32	30	27	24	22	19	17	14	12	9	7	5	2
160	37	36	33	31	28	26	23	20	18	16	13	11	9	6	4	2
170	35	34	31	29	26	24	22	19	17	15	13	10	8	6	4	2
180	32	31	29	27	25	22	20	18	16	14	12	10	8	6	4	2
190	31	30	28	26	24	21	19	17	15	13	11	10	8	6	4	2

RESIDUAL NITROGEN TIMES (MINUTES)

Courtesy of United States Navy

REPETITIVE DIVE WORKSHEET

I. PREVIOUS DIVE:

_____ minutes   ☐ Standard Air Table

_____ feet   ☐ No-Decompression Tab.

_____ repetitive group designation

II. SURFACE INTERVAL:

_____ hours _____ minutes on surface.

Repetitive group from I _____

New repetitive group from surface

Residual Nitrogen Timetable _____

III. RESIDUAL NITROGEN TIME:

_____ feet (depth of repetitive dive)

New repetitive group from II. _____

Residual nitrogen time from

Residual Nitrogen Timetable _____

IV. EQUIVALENT SINGLE DIVE TIME:

_____ minutes, residual nitrogen time from III.

+_____ minutes, actual bottom time of repetitive dive.

=_____ minutes, equivalent single dive time.

V. DECOMPRESSION FOR REPETITIVE DIVE:

_____ minutes, equivalent single dive time from IV.

_____ feet, depth of repetitive dive

Decompression from (check one):
☐ Standard Air Table ☐ No-Decompression Table
☐ Surface Table Using Oxygen ☐ Surface Table Using Air
☐ No decompression required

	Decompression Stops:	_____ feet _____ minutes
		_____ feet _____ minutes
		_____ feet _____ minutes
Schedule used _____		_____ feet _____ minutes
Repetitive group _____		_____ feet _____ minutes

Repetitive Dive Worksheet

Figure 7-2

Courtesy of United States Navy

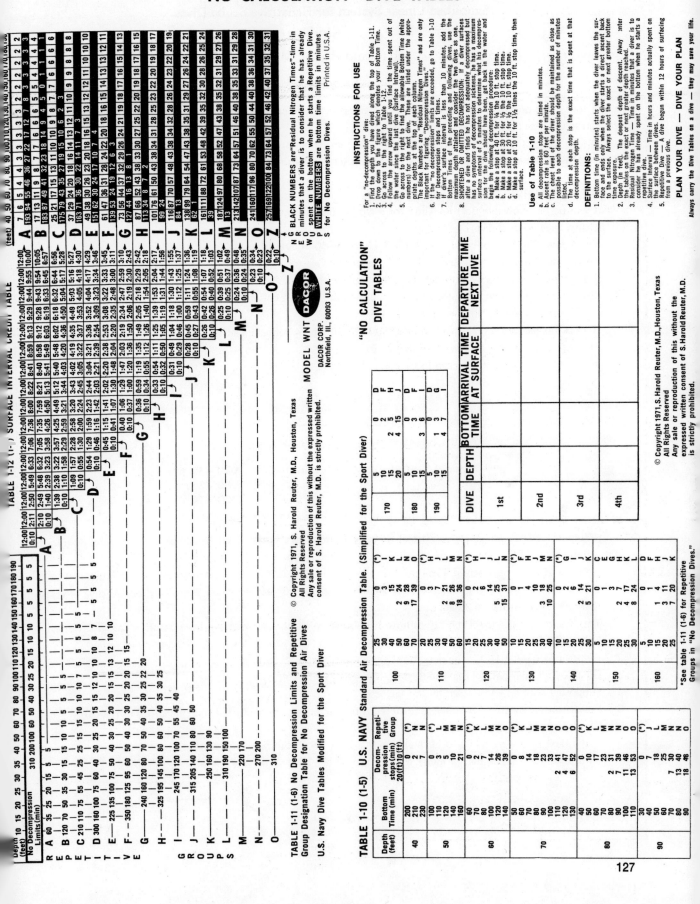

INSTRUCTIONS FOR USE

For a "no-decompression" dive.

1. Find the depth you have dived along the top of Table 1-11.
2. Drop down to the number which denotes your Bottom Time.
3. Go across to the right to Table 1-12.
4. Follow the arrow upward until you find the time spent out of the water since the last dive (Surface Interval).
5. Go across to the right to find the allowable Bottom Time (white numbers) for the next dive. These are listed under the appropriate depths at the top of each column. The Black Numbers are "Residual Nitrogen Times" and are only important for "Decompression Dives."
6. If the "no-decompression" limits are exceeded, go to Table 1-10 for Decompression stops and times.
7. If diver's surface interval is less than 10 minutes, add the Bottom Times of the preceding and following dives, use the maximum depth attained and consider the two dives as one dive.
8. IN COMPRESSION SICKNESS — If, after a dive and finds he has not adequately decompressed but has no symptoms of decompression sickness, he has a maximum surface interval of 5 minutes to determine what his decompression for the dive should have been, get back in the water and begin the following decompression procedure.
   a. Make a stop at 40 ft. for ¼ the 10 ft. stop time.
   b. Make a stop at 30 ft. for ⅓ the 10 ft. stop time.
   c. Make a stop at 20 ft. for ½ the 10 ft. stop time.
   d. Make a stop at 10 ft. for 1½ times the 10 ft. stop time, then surface.

Use of Table 1-10

a. All decompression stops are timed in minutes.
b. Ascent rate is 60 feet per minute.
c. The lowest level of the diver should be maintained as close as possible to each decompression depth for the number of minutes listed.
d. The time at each stop is the exact time that is spent at that decompression depth.

DEFINITIONS:

1. Bottom time (in minutes) starts when the diver leaves the surface and ends only when the diver starts a direct ascent back to the surface. Always select the exact or next greater bottom time exposure.
2. Depth (in feet). The deepest depth of descent. Always enter the tables on the exact or next greater depth reached.
3. Residual Nitrogen Time — Time in minutes that a diver is to consider he has already spent on the bottom when he starts a repetitive dive.
4. Surface Interval — Time in hours and minutes actually spent on the surface between dives.
5. Repetitive Dive — A dive begun within 12 hours of surfacing from a previous dive.

PLAN YOUR DIVE — DIVE YOUR PLAN

Always carry the Dive Tables on a dive — they may save your life.

TABLE 1-11 (1-6) No Decompression Limits and Repetitive Group Designation Table for No Decompression Air Dives

U.S. Navy Dive Tables Modified for the Sport Diver

MODEL WNT
DACOR CORP.
Northfield, Ill., 60093 U.S.A.

TABLE 1-12 (1-7) SURFACE INTERVAL CREDIT TABLE

"NO CALCULATION" DIVE TABLES

TABLE 1-10 (1-5) U.S. NAVY Standard Air Decompression Table. (Simplified for the Sport Diver)

"No-Calculation" Dive Tables
Simplified Linear System for Repetitive Scuba Dives
by
S. Harold Reuter, M.D.

Examples

There are four basic problems for which the U.S. Navy dive tables can provide answers. The "No-Calculation" Linear System can solve these problems very simply and quickly.

Let us consider a hypothetical diver who descends to 50 feet remaining at that depth for 60 minutes (Bottom Time). He then returns to the surface for three hours (Surface Interval) before starting his next dive.

A. FIRST REPETITIVE DIVE (Second Dive)

What will be his allowable Bottom Time for a No-Decompression Dive if he wishes to dive to 70 feet on his first Repetitive Dive (second dive)?

1. Drop down the 50 foot column in Table 1-11 to the 60 minute line.
2. Go across to the right to Table 1-12 ("H" Repetitive Group).
3. Follow the arrow upward until reaching the limits within which three hours falls (2:24 to 3:20).
4. Go across to the right ("D" Repetitive Group) to the 70 foot column where the Bottom Time limit is found to be 30 minutes (White Number—Black Background).

   This is the maximum time that can be spent without having to make Decompression Stops.

   If less time was spent, proceed to Example B.

   If more time was spent, proceed to Example C.

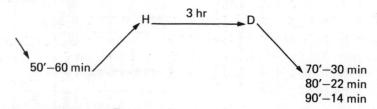

B. SECOND REPETITIVE DIVE (Third Dive)

If the Repetitive Dive was made to 70 feet for only 15 minutes Bottom Time instead of the maximum 30 minutes allowed, how would the tables be used to determine the next Repetitive Dive (third dive)?

1. Add the 15 minutes Bottom Time used on the second dive to the 20 minutes Bottom Time which is the time that a diver is to consider that he has already spent at 70 feet when he *starts* the second dive (Residual Nitrogen Time)—totaling 35 minutes.

   This Residual Nitrogen Time (20 minutes) is shown in Black figures above the Bottom Time limits in White figures (30 minutes).

2. Returning to Table 1-11, drop down the 70 foot column to 35 minutes.
3. Go across to the right to enter the Surface Interval Credit Table as a "G" Diver.
4. Suppose 1 hour was now spent on the surface.
5. Follow the arrow after "G" upward until reaching the limits within which 1 hour falls (0:41 to 1:15).
6. Go across to the right to become an "F" Diver.
7. If the next dive were made to 50 feet, the maximum No-Decompression Bottom Time would be 53 minutes (White Number—Black Background). For a 60 foot dive, 24 minutes or 70 foot dive, 19 minutes.

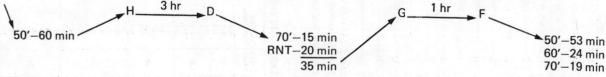

C. DECOMPRESSION REPETITIVE DIVE

How does the diver determine his Decompression Stops if he finds his Bottom Time at 70 feet is 55 minutes instead of the maximum 30 minutes allowed?

1. Add the 55 minutes Bottom Time used on the second dive to the 20 minutes Bottom Time which is the time that a diver is to consider he has already spent at 70 feet when he *starts* the second dive (Residual Nitrogen Time)—totaling 75 minutes.
2. Go to Table 1-10 Standard Air Decompression Table.
3. In the Depth Column locate 70 feet.
4. Go across to the right, in the 80 minute line (exact or next greatest Bottom Time) to find that a 18 minute Decompression Stop is necessary at 10 feet.
5. The letter next to 18 is "M" which indicates a new Repetitive Group Designation following decompression.
6. Suppose 2 hours were now spent on the surface.
7. Enter Table 1-12 following the arrow after "M" upward until reaching the limits within which 2 hours falls (1:40 to 2:05).
8. Go across to the right to become an "H" Diver.
9. If the next dive were made to 50 feet, the maximum No-Decompression Bottom Time would be 34 minutes (White Number—Black Background). For a 60 foot dive, 8 minutes or 70 foot dive, 7 minutes.

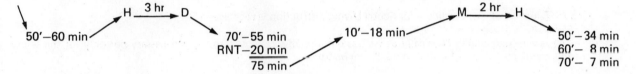

D. SURFACE INTERVAL FOR NO-DECOMPRESSION REPETITIVE DIVE

Suppose the diver wishes to go to 70 feet for this first Repetitive Dive (second dive) for a Bottom Time of 40 minutes without the necessity of decompression stops? The proper Surface Interval must now be determined.

1. Enter Table 1-11 at the 50 foot column dropping down to 60 minutes (as in problem A).
2. Go across to the right to find the Repetitive Group which is "H".
3. Leave this table remembering the Group Designation and go to Table 1-13 in the 70 foot column.
4. Dropping down to the exact Bottom Time desired (40 minutes), or the next greater, stop at the 41 minute Bottom Time limit line which is in the "B" Group line.
5. Go to the left until the "H" column is reached. The minimal Surface Interval for a No-Decompression Dive is found to be 4 hours and 50 minutes.

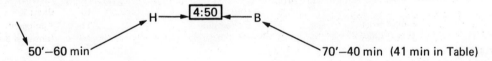

Plan Your Dive — Dive Your Plan

Always carry the Dive Tables on a dive — they may save your life.

APPENDIX E

SKIN AND SCUBA DIVING MEDICAL REPORT

Basic Medical Examination Form

To the Candidate for Scuba Instruction:

Please print or type and complete medical history on reverse side:

Name_____ Age:_____ Sex: Male_____ Female_____
Address_____ City _____ State _____ Zip _____
Home Phone:_____ Occupation: _____
Weight:_____ pounds: Height_____feet _____ Inches.

TO THE EXAMINING PHYSICIAN:

Dear Doctor:

Your evaluation of this candidate for Scuba Diving instruction is requested.

Diving is very demanding physically as well as emotionally. Utmost stability is necessary not only for the safety of this candidate but also for that of his diving buddies.

The following sets forth minimal requirements which should be expanded by further evaluation and testing as you deem necessary. Examination of candidates over 40 years of age should include an electrocardiogram with exercise and full chest X-ray as well as a thorough physical examination.

S. Harold Reuter, MD

S. Harold Reuter, M.D.
Medical Advisor
National YMCA Scuba Program.

PHYSICIAN'S GUIDE TO MEDICAL EXAMINATION:

A.   Medical History: See reverse side for candidate's history.
B.   Examination:

_____ 1	Head & Neck	_____ 5	Lungs & Chest	_____ 9	Psychiatric
_____ 2	Eyes	_____ 6	Heart	_____ 10	Chest X-ray
_____ 3	Ears, Nose, Throat	_____ 7	Extremities	_____ 11	Audiogram
_____ 4	Back & Abdomen	_____ 8	Neurologic		(optional but advisable)

C.   Comments on Examination: _____
_____
_____

D.   Conclusion:
_____APPROVAL for diving.
_____DISAPPROVAL—candidate unfit for Scuba Diving.
Reason: _____
Possible Correction: _____

Signature: _____M.D.

Office Address: _____

Date: _____   Phone: _____

130

Medical History

To the Candidate for Scuba Instruction:

Skin and Scuba Diving are very demanding physically, mentally, and emotionally, requiring that the participant be in top condition.

Prior to your medical examination, complete the top of the reverse side and the Medical History below. (Please type or print.)

Check appropriate number and explain in detail below.

Save your Physician time by being brief but complete.

_____ 1.	Medical Problems	
_____ 2.	Recent Illnesses	
_____ 3.	Operations	
_____ 4.	Physical Handicaps	
_____ 5.	Mental or Emotional Problems	
_____ 6.	Medications taken regularly	
_____ 7.	Allergies (List Drugs Taken)	
_____ 8.	Respiratory Problems	
_____ 9.	Hayfever, Asthma or Bronchitis	
_____ 10.	Difficulty Breathing through the Nose	
_____ 11.	Shortness of Breath	
_____ 12.	Persistent Cough	
_____ 13.	Frequent Colds or Sore Throats	
_____ 14.	Sinus Trouble	
_____ 15.	Headaches	
_____ 16.	Ear or Face Pain when going to the bottom of the swimming pool	

_____ 17. Ear Trouble (Pain, Drainage, Rupture)
_____ 18. Ear Pain with change of altitude
_____ 19. Hearing Loss
_____ 20. Rheumatic Fever
_____ 21. Heart Trouble or Palpitations
_____ 22. Chest Pain
_____ 23. Epilepsy, Fits or Convulsions
_____ 24. Diabetes (List Medications)
_____ 25. Dizziness, Fainting or Motion Sickness
_____ 26. Claustrophobia (Fear of closed-in spaces)
_____ 27. Panic easily
_____ 28. Glasses or Contacts
_____ 29. Alcoholic Beverages: _____Occasional _____Heavy
_____ 30. Smoke _____packs per day
_____ 31. Rejection from any activity for Medical reasons
_____ 32. Medical Problems Not listed

EXPLANATIONS: (Please type or Print.) _____

_____

_____

DATES OF LAST:
Chest X-ray _____
Electrocardiogram _____

Medical Examination _____
Hearing Test _____
Tetanus Immunization _____

I have read thoroughly and completed the above to the best of my knowledge and certify that I have not withheld any information.

Candidate's Signature _____

If candidate is under 21 years of age, parent must participate in completion of above, give permission for Scuba instruction, and have signature witnessed.

Date:_____

Parent's Signature _____

Witness _____

INDEX

ABOUT THE AUTHOR

Joe Strykowski is the producer-host of the television series "Man and Sea."

His camera has been his passport to diving adventure around the world. He is a formidable film-maker and his underwater and vanishing wildlife film work has received wide television coverage.

Since his first published work appeared in a national magazine at age 14, he has been writer, correspondent, editor and photo-journalist whose photographs and stories have appeared in scores of periodicals.

A former working diver, he is also a well-qualified engineer having worked on the development of much new underwater equipment, most recently as project engineer in the development of a complete saturation diving complex.

Joe Strykowski was one of the pioneers of diving safety and his credentials are numerous. He was one of the very first instructors to be nationally certified and the divers he has introduced to the underwater world number in the thousands.

Joe is a board member of the Marine Technology Society, National YMCA Scuba Committee and the Gillette Scuba Safety Association and serves as a diver training consultant to the undersea industry. Joe is a member of the American Society of Mechanical Engineers, Outdoor Writers Association of America and the American Society for Oceanography.

It is from this diversified underwater background that Joe Strykowski has provided the material and proven methods included in this book.

Friday after 12:00 PM
Before 9:00 PM

Fedral Way

I 5 towards Seattle
143 exit 320th St F.W.